Legal Forms,
Contracts,
and Advice for
Horse Owners

Legal Forms, Contracts, and Advice for Horse Owners

Sue Ellen Marder, L.L.M.
and
Judith B. Oakes, J.D.

 Breakthrough Publications

Acknowledgment

The publisher wishes to thank S. W. "Woody" Longan, III, attorney-at-law in Missouri and Kansas, for his editorial review during development of this new edition.

For information address:
Breakthrough Publications, Inc.
Ossining, New York 10562
www.booksonhorses.com

ISBN: 0-914327-69-0

Library of Congress Catalog Card Number: 96-79601

03 02 01 00 99 98
2 3 4 5 6 7 8 9 0

Contents

How to Use This Book

This book aims to inform people how they may protect themselves in horse-related business contracts. Too often horse transactions are conducted verbally and the final agreement is never written down. Each person may walk away from the deal with a different understanding of what was said. Even more frequently, the parties involved may not anticipate the consequences of the arrangement or unforeseen situations that may intervene. Those who have had any experience with horses know that the old axiom, "what can go wrong does go wrong," was never truer. This book may ease the horse owner through those problems, avoiding lawsuits, financial loss, and hurt feelings.

Horses have become big business in this country. Breeding, raising, racing, showing, and selling horses require a tremendous capital outlay and are subject to many financial and personal considerations. This book cannot cover the many intricacies individual situations may present. Some of the transactions discussed are complicated, and the advice of an attorney should *always* be sought to ascertain the long-range effects as well as the short-term benefits of planning decisions. This book, however, should make horse owners or investors more aware of their options and suggest areas of complexity that require documentation to reduce their potential liability.

Included in each chapter are sample forms that illustrate the most general and frequent uses of the basic legal contract. At the end of the book is a selection of blank forms of the more routine legal contracts.

The sample forms and the blank forms are supplied merely as **samples,** and **they are not meant to replace legal counsel.** The forms try to follow a middle ground, that is they reflect the basic needs of both parties, for example, a buyer **and** a seller. Often there are unique personal considerations or legislation that will alter the standard contract. Much of the time the reader will require a contract or agreement that reflects his or her particular situation and, therefore, should consult an attorney to discuss the contents of any legally binding document.

For example, a novice and first-time purchaser of a horse may wish to contract to buy a horse from a professional dealer. The sample buy-sell agreement in this book does not address the disparity in experience and remedies available to the novice on the one hand and the experienced horse dealer on the other. An attorney can help the reader to draft a contract that will protect both parties and yet be acceptable to both.

Whenever a contract involves a minor, such as in a release for a minor's riding lessons, special legal issues arise. There is a separate body of law that pertains to minors. Each state's law varies, not only as to what constitutes a minor, but also to what legal safeguards exist for a minor. Therefore, it is advisable to consult an attorney concerning your state's laws before drafting any contract involving a minor.

Chapter 1 addresses the important topic of release and hold harmless agreements and the National Equine Liability Laws that have been and are being enacted in many states. It is very important that readers find out about these laws in their particular state and whether they impact their equine activities. Liens and lien enforcement is discussed in Chapter 2—another important section to read.

Chapter 3 is a discussion of the different ways of forming a horse business and describes the advantages and disadvantages of the sole proprietorship; limited and general partnerships; the corporation and the S corporation; and syndications. Individual case studies are included with some of the legal forms for illustrative purposes. In the chapters that follow the sample agreements are relevant whether the individual is operating as a sole proprietor or within a partnership or a corporation.

Each of the chapters that follow describes a legal form and its use, often with a description of a typical situation that might face a rider, horse owner, or investor. The sample form has been filled in based on the needs of one person in a particular circumstance, and the reader must always bear this in mind. The form is followed by a thorough point-by-point discussion of the terms in the contract.

Common Questions on Legal Forms

Here are six questions that are most often asked about legal forms with brief answers to each. In fact, this entire book is devoted to answering questions such as these.

Q. *When is an agreement a legally binding contract?*

A. A contract is an agreement between two or more persons that creates an obligation to do or not to do a particular thing. You are in a legally binding contract at the point you commit the agreement to a signed writing and some form of payment or an exchange of goods or services, called "consideration," has passed between you. A contract to be binding must name the parties, subject matter, consideration (payment), and agreement of parties to perform their obligations.

The consideration, usually money, may be a small token of the entire transaction. No minimum percent is required. There is nothing in law that says the consideration has to be "reasonable."

Q. *Is it possible to create a contract without having it in writing?*

A. Yes, if certain factors are present. You have a contract if one person has made promises and the second person has relied on those promises to his detriment (suffered some kind of damage or given up something). In this event, the first person is now obligated as if a written contract had been signed. This is where disputes can arise, because each person's memory of a conversation may be different.

Reminder: Get everything in writing.

Q. *Does it matter which party writes the contract?*

A. The party that writes the contract has a definite advantage. You may write it yourself (with the help of this book) or you can hire a lawyer to write it. It may seem like more work or expense at the time to prepare the contract yourself, but the party that writes it has a definite advantage. The writer provides the clauses he/she wants with the most advantageous wording. The other party has the opportunity to request changes, but often the document retains the flavor (or bias) of the person who drafts it. There is no underhandedness here, but this procedure will best protect your interests. However, in the event of a dispute over the interpretation or terms of a contract, the terms will be construed *against* the drafting party.

If you do seek help from a lawyer, first write down all the issues that are important to you to make sure that they are covered in the final agreement. A lawyer cannot anticipate all your concerns.

Sometimes both parties may draft contracts, and these can form the basis of negotiation and compromise. In other words, knowing where you both start, you can work toward a middle ground.

Too often, a person signs a paper without fully reading it or understanding its impact. That won't happen to you if you or your representative wrote it.

Q. *Is there any special wording required in an agreement?*

A. No, the more precise the language, the more likely it will not be misinterpreted or create issues that might be disputed at a later date.

Q. *What is the most common weakness of many contracts?*

A. They are overly simplistic. Neither side anticipates the possible contingencies in the event the business transaction does not go as planned. Consulting a legal professional about legal matters or a professional in the horse business for horse-related questions will clarify the possible problems that may arise. This ensures that all angles are covered within the agreement and saves legal fees and irritation later.

Q. *What are the basic elements of a written agreement?*

A. The following is a checklist of items to be considered when preparing an agreement. Terms can be added or deleted, depending upon the nature of the contract:

- Names and full addresses of all parties
- Description of the horse(s) if applicable
- Purpose of agreement
- Date of delivery, or point at which contract begins
- Duration of agreement
- Financial terms of agreement
- Payment of additional expenses
- Care of the horse
- Release and hold harmless
- Risk of loss if the horse dies or if someone is hurt
- Arbitration of disputes
- Indemnification (who is entitled to reimbursement if someone is sued)
- Termination of agreement: grounds, notice
- Governing law or arbitration
- Date of agreement
- Signatures

Each of these terms will be discussed in more detail within the following chapters.

1

Release and Hold Harmless Agreements: National Equine Activity Liability Laws

A liability release, which states that the person or business being released from liability will be held legally harmless in the event of an injury, is common to many types of agreements, such as those involving boarding, training, lessons, and horse and facility rental, whether involving a professional or, in some cases, even where the exchange of money is not involved.

National equine liability laws have been enacted in many states. As of summer 1996, thirty-six states had enacted such legislation. These laws usually contain one or both of two different requirements: a "sign" requirement and a "release" requirement. Their purpose is to limit or control certain liabilities in cases where personal injuries arise from equine-related activities. Before drafting any contract or agreement that should contain a release or hold harmless clause, you should determine whether your state has now enacted an equine activity liability law that dictates the language to be used in such documents.

You will want to determine if your equine-related activity falls within the category where a warning sign must be posted and, if so, what exact language must be used in the sign.

The states having a sign requirement require that certain segments of the horse industry, mainly involving equine professionals, must post conspicuous warning signs using language as provided in the statute. Many of these laws also regulate the size of the lettering of the signs and others regulate the color of the signs as well.

Those states having the release requirement often, but not always, require that the same language required for the sign warnings also be used in various contracts commonly containing release provisions, particularly those used by equine professionals for the rental or provision of horses, rental of equipment, and/or providing professional services such as training, lessons, and boarding.

Each state's law on equine activity liability varies, so it is imperative that you contact an attorney who is licensed to practice in your state, or obtain a copy of the law of your state yourself by contacting your state legislator, your local library, or through your state horse council or agricultural extension service.

To illustrate the wide differences in requirement under these laws, partial language from the laws of two states, Kansas and Illinois, are set forth below merely as examples.

As to the release language requirement, in part:

Kansas

Under Kansas law, there is no liability for an injury to or the death of a participant in domestic animal activities resulting from the inherent risk of domestic animal activities pursuant to (sections of contract). Inherent risks of domestic animal activities include but shall not be limited to: (1) the propensity of a domestic animal to behave in ways, i.e., running, bucking, biting, kicking, shying, stumbling, rearing, falling or stepping on that may result in an injury, harm, or death to persons on or around them; (2) the unpredictability of a domestic animal's reaction to such things as sound, sudden movements, and unfamiliar objects, persons, or other animals; (3) certain hazards such as surface or subsurface conditions; (4) collisions with other domestic animals or objects; and (5) the potential of a participant to act in a negligent manner that may contribute to injury to the participant or others such as failing to maintain control over the domestic animal or not acting within a participant's ability. You are assuming the risk of participating in this domestic activity.

As to the warning requirement, in part:

Illinois

Under the Equine Activity Liability Act, each participant who engages in an equine activity expressly assumes the risk of engaging in and legal responsibility for injury, loss, or damage to person or property resulting from the risk of equine activities.

Liability issues are serious in the equine industry. An established stable or breeding facility could be forced to close as a result of one personal injury incident. The language necessary to protect an individual or business entity from liability for ordinary negligence is complex, and an attorney should be consulted to prepare documents with the relevant language.

2

Liens and Lien Enforcement

A lien is a right to retain possession of property until a debt is satisfied.

A right of lien clause should be placed in every contract where the scenario exists for one party to the contract to be left with the custody and/or care of the horse belonging to the other party to the contract, or when one party can be left with unpaid bills incurred by the other party. A typical example is the boarding contract wherein the owner of the boarding facility has incurred considerable expenses in the care and feeding of the boarder's horse, possibly even including farrier and veterinary care. The boarder, for one reason or another, is behind in payments or fails to pay his board. A right of lien clause will enable the stable owner to place a lien on the horse in the event that the owner does not pay his or her bill.

The process of enforcing an animal lien, in most states, is not as simple as a mechanic's lien on a car. Proper notice usually must be given the debtor. Also the owner of the horse needs an opportunity to divest his or her interest in the horse so that the horse may be sold without recourse to judicial proceedings. Only after all these steps have been taken may the creditor apply to the court for an order to sell the horse. Even then, the debtor has an opportunity and right to be heard before the court will order such a sale. Unlike an automobile, the creditor does not usually wish to hold on to a horse for an indefinite period since the costs of care keep mounting. Thus, if the debtor cannot pay the amount due quickly, the creditor will wish to sell the horse and both recover his past losses and cut future losses. A properly written agreement can avoid this situation.

Before drafting a right to lien clause in a contract, it is important to consult the law of your state in regard to livestock or equine liens.

3

Different Ways of Doing Business

Choosing the best method (and contract) for operating a horse business is a complex decision. Sometimes the business evolves naturally, based on the owner's needs and priorities, but usually this area requires good professional counseling because every business and business contract has legal consequences. The Tax Reform Act of 1986 and its subsequent revisions have further complicated this area. (See companion book, L. A. Winter and S. E. Marder, *Tax Planning and Preparation for Horse Owners*, Breakthrough Publications, 1996.)

In general, start the simplest type of business and use the simplest contract possible under the circumstances. The catch is obvious: Circumstances may dictate a more complex business form than would be normally required. Many different business arrangements can be made, but we are now going to examine several of the most common, including sole proprietorships and partnerships.

The following descriptions of various ways of doing business are intended for general informational purposes only. There are both benefits and drawbacks and/or risks attached to each of the entities described below. A particular set of facts and circumstances will determine which entity is best in a certain situation. It is strongly advised that professional advice and assistance be sought before selecting any of the following business arrangements. Only a professional knowledgeable in all aspects of tax and corporate law will be able to determine which entity is proper for a particular case.

SOLE PROPRIETORSHIP

The simplest type of business is the sole proprietorship. One person owns the business. Usually the person with the knowledge and skill manages the business alone and puts in his or her own money.

> **Example.** Nancy B. wants to open a riding stable. She has saved $10,000 to cover start-up costs. She already owns a few school horses and a six-stall barn with several paddocks and a ring. As an experienced show rider, she plans to instruct riders and train horses.

The sole proprietorship is a practical way of doing business for Nancy. She has the necessary expertise to run the business herself and wants to keep the business small. Her funds are limited, but enough to cover start-up costs. At this point, she doesn't want the additional expense of incorporation. She will file her personal tax return with Schedule F, since she is running a farm and is self-employed.

Liability

Because Nancy is personally liable for what happens on her farm, she takes out an insurance policy covering her personal liability in case someone is injured on the property. In addition, she has informed herself thoroughly of the National Equine Activity Liability laws in the state where she plans to start her business. She will post signs in accordance with those laws and have a lawyer help her draw up a release form to be signed by each parent and rider. The form states that the person who signs recognizes the risks inherent in all horse-related activities and will not sue the owner of the farm or the instructor for any injuries connected with the riding program. (See Chapter 1, "Release and Hold Harmless Agreements.")

However, it must be cautioned that should an accident occur and the damages exceed the amount of the insurance policy, or if punitive damages are added to the actual damages suffered, the injured party may seek additional compensation through the court from Nancy's personal assets such as her family farm, her automobile, and her horses. Unlike other entities described below, as a sole proprietor, Nancy's liability is not limited.

PARTNERSHIP

A partnership exists under the Tax Code when two or more people carry on any form of business with each person contributing money, property, labor, or skill, and all members expecting to share in the profits and losses (Code Sec. 761).

> **Example.** Silas M. and Jenny W., both experienced stable managers and riders, decide to go into business buying and selling show horses. They plan to pool their savings and share all responsibilities of this new venture. Silas and Jenny are in business together. They are contributing money, labor, and skill, and both plan to share profits and losses. By definition, they are not sole proprietors but are partners.

The partnership form of operating a horse business has become increasingly popular with the rising price of horses and the costs of racing, breeding, or showing. It provides the means to spread expenses and risks, but with its growing use have come increasingly complex tax rules affecting partnerships.

Although a partnership is not taxed as such, its taxable income for the year must be computed and an information return must be filed reporting the partnership income, expenses, gains, and losses. This taxable income is then divided among the partners and reported by each partner on his individual return.

Liability

The partnership arrangement does not provide any more protection from liability than does the sole proprietorship.

Electing Not to Be Taxed as a Partnership

Under certain circumstances, all members of a partnership may elect not to be treated as partners, i.e., to file returns as individuals without the partnership information form. To make such an election, the partnership must be formed solely for investment purposes or for the purpose of using property without selling services or selling the property produced. Most horse businesses do not fit within these exceptions.

Sometimes a stallion breeding partnership is formed for servicing the mares of partners. In this case, a statement would be attached to the partnership information tax return for the first year. After that, the partners would file as individuals without the partnership return.

Rules on Business Participation

As a partner or sole proprietor, the investor in the horse business must face passive loss limitations. This means that if the person is not actively involved in the horse business, the losses from this activity will not be allowed to offset income from a salary, business, or investment portfolio (for instance, dividends).

Generally, all work done in connection with the business, from mucking stalls to attending horse shows to evaluating a horse's performance, counts toward hours spent in the business. Horses don't respect office hours, so the twelve- to sixteen-hour day is unfortunately not uncommon. The surest way to qualify as an active partner is to participate in the activity for more than 500 hours during the year, but an individual can also qualify with more than 100 hours during the year as long as he or she participates on a regular, continuous, and substantive basis.

Nancy B., the sole proprietor, as well as Silas M. and Jenny W., the partners, easily qualify as active participants in their businesses. The care and management of horses is highly labor intensive.

On the other hand, an investor who provides money but hires others to run the business will probably fail the test for active participation. If the taxpayer does not put in the requisite hours, he or she will not be able to deduct horse business losses from other income such as salary or dividends and interest.

The following form is the partnership agreement entered into by Silas M. and Jenny W. Theirs is a very basic agreement stating their purpose to buy and sell horses, along with an allocation of their financial interests.

PARTNERSHIP AGREEMENT

THE PARTNERSHIP AGREEMENT is made this _____ day of _____ (month), _____ (year), by and between ___ Jenny W. ___ and ___ Silas M. ___.

EXPLANATORY STATEMENT

The parties hereto desire to enter into the business of __purchasing, acquiring, owning, and selling horses and ponies and engaging in any other lawful phase or aspect of the horse business.__
In order to accomplish their aforesaid desires, the parties hereto desire to join together in a general partnership under and pursuant to any applicable state code.

NOW, THEREFORE, in consideration of their mutual promises, covenants, and agreements, and the Explanatory Statement, which is incorporated by reference herein and made a substantive part of this Partnership Agreement, the parties hereto do hereby promise, covenant, and agree as follows:

Section 1. Name.

The name of the partnership shall be _____ "Centaur Associates."

Section 2. Principal Place of Business.

The principal place of business of the Partnership (the "Office") shall be located at
101 Stable Street
Partners, MD

Section 3. Business and Purpose.

3.1 The business and purposes of the Partnership are to ___ acquire, hold, manage, sell, and lease horses and ponies (the "Property"), or interests therein, and to engage in any other phase or aspect of the horse business.

3.2 The Partnership may also do and engage in any and all other things and activities and have all powers incident to the said acquisition, holding, management, sale, and leasing of the Property, or any part or parts thereof.

Section 4. Term.

The Partnership shall commence upon the date of the Agreement, as set forth above, and shall terminate pursuant to the further provisions of this Agreement.

Section 5. Capital Contributions.

5.1 The original capital contributions to the Partnership of each of the Partners shall be made concurrently with their respective execution of this Agreement in the following dollar amounts set forth after their respective names:

Jenny W. _____ $ _____
Silas M. _____ $ _____

5.2 An individual capital account shall be maintained for each Partner. The capital account of each Partner shall consist of his or her original capital contribution, increased by (a) additional capital contributions made by him or her, and (b) his or her share of Partnership profits, and decreased by (i) distributions of such profits and capital to him or her, and (ii) his or her share of Partnership losses.

5.3 Except as specifically provided in this Agreement, or as otherwise provided by and in accordance with law to the extent such law is not inconsistent with this Agreement, no Partner shall have the right to withdraw or reduce his or her contributions to the capital of the Partnership.

Section 6. Profit and Loss.

6.1 The percentages of Partnership Rights and Partnership Interest of each of the Partners in the Partnership shall be as follows:

Jenny W. _____ 50%
Silas M. _____ 50%

6.2 For purposes of Sections 702 and 704 of the Internal Revenue Code of 1986, or the corresponding provisions of any future federal

Internal Revenue law, or any similar tax law of any state or jurisdiction, the determination of each Partner's distributive share of all items of income, gain, loss, deduction, credit, or allowance of the Partnership for any period or year shall be made in accordance with, and in proportion to, such Partner's percentage of Partnership Interest as it may then exist.

Section 7. Distribution of Profits.

The net cash from operations of the Partnership shall be distributed at such times as may be determined by the Partners in accordance with Section 8 of this Agreement among the Partners in proportion to their respective percentage of Partnership Interest.

Section 8. Management of the Partnership Business.

8.1 All decisions respecting the management, operation, and control of the Partnership business and determinations made in accordance with the provisions of this Agreement shall be made only by the unanimous vote or consent of all of the Partners.

8.2 The Partners shall devote to the conduct of the Partnership business as much of their respective time as may be reasonably necessary for the efficient operation of the Partnership business.

Section 9. Salaries.

Unless otherwise agreed by the Partners in accordance with Section 8 of this Agreement, no partner shall receive any salary for services rendered to or for the Partnership.

Section 10. Legal Title to Partnership Property.

Legal title to the property of the Partnership shall be held in the name of ___Centaur Associates___ or in such other name or manner as the Partners shall determine to be in the best interest of the Partnership.

Section 11. Banking.

All revenue of the Partnership shall be deposited regularly in the Partnership savings and checking accounts at such bank or banks as shall be selected by the Partners.

Section 12. Books; Fiscal Year.

Accurate and complete books of account shall be kept by the Partners and entries promptly made therein of all of the transactions of the Partnership, and such books of account shall be open at all times to the inspection and examination of the Partners.

Section 13. Transfer of Partnership Interest and Partnership Rights.

Except as otherwise provided in Sections 14, 15, and 16 hereof, no Partner (hereinafter referred to as the "Offering Partner") shall, during the term of the Partnership, sell, hypothecate, pledge, assign, or otherwise transfer with or without consideration (hereinafter collectively referred to as a "Transfer") any part or all of his Partnership Interest or Partnership Rights in the Partnership to any other person (a "Transferee"), without first offering (hereinafter referred to as the "Offer") that portion of his Partnership Interest and Partnership Rights in the Partnership subject to the contemplated transfer (hereinafter referred to as the "Offered Interest") first to the Partnership, and, secondly, to the other Partners, at a purchase price (hereinafter referred to as the "Transfer Purchase Price") and in a manner as agreed.

Section 14. Purchase upon Death.

14.1 Upon the death of any Partner (hereinafter referred to as the "Decedent") the Partnership shall neither be terminated nor wound up, but instead, the business of the Partnership shall be continued as if such death had not occurred. Each Partner shall have the right of testamentary disposition to bequeath all or any portion of his Partnership Interest and Partnership Rights in the Partnership to a member of his immediate family or to any trust in which any one or more members of the immediate family retain the full beneficial interests.

14.2 The aggregate dollar amount of the Decedent Purchase Price shall be payable in cash on the closing date, unless the Partnership shall elect prior to or on the closing date to purchase the Decedent Interest in installments as provided in Section 19 hereof.

Section 15. Purchase upon Bankruptcy or Retirement.

15.1 Upon the Bankruptcy or Retirement from the Partnership of any Partner (the "Withdrawing Partner"), the Partnership shall neither be terminated nor wound up, but, instead, the business of the Partnership shall be continued as if such Bankruptcy or Retirement, as the case may be, had not occurred, and the Partnership shall purchase and the Withdrawing Partner shall sell all of the Partnership Interest and Partnership Rights (the "Withdrawing Partner's Interest") owned by the Withdrawing Partner in the Partnership on the date of such Bankruptcy or Retirement (the "Withdrawal Date").

Section 16. The Appraised Value.

The term "Appraised Value," as used in this Agreement, shall be the dollar amount equal to the product obtained by multiplying (a) the percentage of Partnership Interest and Partnership Rights owned by a Partner by (b) the Fair Market Value of the Partnership's assets.

Section 17. Notices.

Any and all notices, offers, acceptances, requests, certifications, and consents provided for in this Agreement shall be in writing and shall be given and be deemed to have been given when personally delivered against a signed receipt or mailed by registered or certified mail, return receipt requested, to the last address which the addressee has given to the Partnership.

Section 18. (a) Governing Law.

It is the intent of the parties hereto that all questions with respect to the construction of this Agreement and rights, duties, obligations, and liabilities of the parties shall be determined in accordance with the applicable provisions of the laws of the State of ___Maryland___
Any legal action must be brought in _____
_____ (county/municipality).

OR

(b) Arbitration.

The parties to this Agreement mutually agree that any and all disputes arising in connection with this Agreement shall be settled and determined by binding arbitration conducted in accordance with the then existing rules of the Americn Arbitration Association by one or more arbitrators appointed in accordance with said rules. Said arbitration shall take place in
_____ (municipality)
_____ (state).

Section 19. Miscellaneous Provisions.

19.1 This Agreement shall be binding upon, and inure to the benefit of, all parties hereto, their personal and legal representatives, guardians, successors, and their assigns to the extent, but only to the extent, that assignment is provided for in accordance with, and permitted by, the provisions of this Agreement.

19.2 Nothing herein contained shall be construed to limit in any manner the parties, or their respective agents, servants, and employees, in carrying on their own respective business or activities.

19.3 The Partners agree that they and each of them will take whatever actions as are deemed by counsel to the Partnership to be reasonably necessary or desirable from time to time to effectuate the provisions or intent of this Agreement.

19.4 This Agreement and exhibits attached hereto set forth all (and are intended by all parties hereto to be an integration of all) of the promises, agreements, conditions, understandings, warranties, and representations among the parties hereto with respect to the Partnership, the business of the Partnership, and the property of the Partnership, and there are no promises, agreements, conditions, understandings, warranties or representations, oral or written, express or implied, among them other than as set forth herein.

Section 20. Entire Agreement.

This constitutes the entire Agreement between the parties. Any modifications or additions MUST be in writing and signed by all parties to this Agreement. No oral modifications or additions will be considered to be part of this Agreement unless reduced to writing and signed by all parties.

　　IN WITNESS WHEREOF, the parties have hereunto set their hands and seals and acknowledged this Agreement as of the date first above written.

WITNESS:　　　　　　　Percentage of Partnership Interest and Partnership Rights

_____
Jenny W.

_____ (SEAL) ___50____ %

Residence Address:_____

_____

_____

_____

_____
Silas M.

_____ (SEAL) ___50____ %

Residence Address: _____

_____

_____

_____

　　IN WITNESS WHEREOF, I have hereunto set my hand and seal as of the date first above written.

WITNESS: _____

_____ (SEAL)

Discussion of Sample Partnership Agreement

This general partnership agreement may seem complicated, but in fact, it has been simplified. Most fledgling partnerships will require professional counsel because there are several complex issues to resolve.

The agreement begins with the date and the names of the partners.

The Explanatory Statement describes the purpose of the agreement in general terms. The relevant body of state law is also alluded to here. The following sections are the basic elements of the agreement:

1. The name of the partnership is stated.

2. The place of business is given with a full address.

3. The general purpose of the business is stated, in this case to sell and lease horses and ponies. The powers necessary to engage in this business are given to the partners.

4. The term of the agreement can be set here. In this example, the date of termination is indefinite.

5. This section clarifies the financial commitments by listing the capital contributions. In addition, the system of accounting for each partner's interest is described.

6. The percentages of each partner's interest is designated as 50%. Each partner will receive his or her profits and losses based on this percent.

7. The profits will be distributed at times designated by the partners. At this point in most partnership agreements, there would be a detailed definition of net cash and taxable income for federal income tax purposes.

8. All agreements made by the partnership require a unanimous vote or consent of both members. They both agree to devote as much time to the business as necessary.

9. No partner receives a salary. They receive distributions of profits instead.

10. All legal title of partnership property is held in the name of the partnership unless they agree otherwise.

11. The partnership maintains a separate bank account.

12. The books must be kept accurately and are open to each partner's inspection.

13. One partner cannot transfer his interest without first giving the other partner the option to buy him out. The transfer purchase price based on the appraised value can be a very complex section including the determination of appraised value and the rules for selling an interest.

14. The transfer of the interest on death can be highly complex, stating the procedures for heirs to notify other partners and the procedure for purchasing the decedent's interest. The partnership can be terminated in the event of a death.

15. The purchase upon bankruptcy or retirement is another option which requires one partner to sell his interest to the other partner(s). The procedure for this sale can be set out in full detail.

16. The appraised value is explained in a deceivingly simple formula, but this is a very complex calculation better left to professionals.

17. All notices must be in writing personally delivered or sent by certified mail.

18. The state of governing law and the location (venue) for any legal action is named, or the parties may agree to arbitration should any dispute arise.

19. Under miscellaneous provisions, this agreement shall be binding on any person who receives a partnership interest through one of the existing partners.

Nothing in the agreement should control how the individual partners run another business.

This agreement is intended as an integration of all verbal statements and stands as the sole agreement.

Some agreements include requirements that each partner has a will authorizing the execution of the partnership interest as stated in the agreement.

Finally, the agreement is signed by each partner and the percent of his partnership interest and his address is noted. It is witnessed by another person.

This general partnership agreement is meant only as a sample to help the reader better understand the general nature and scope of the form.

LIMITED PARTNERSHIP

A limited partnership is one in which one or more partners have limited liability. Limited liability means a partner's losses cannot exceed a predetermined amount. If the business were to be sued, the partner would not bear the cost beyond this set figure. In addition, a limited partnership must have one or more general partners who do not have limited liability and who normally manage the partnership.

Example: Marielle has the expertise to run a riding stable business. Several of her wealthy friends would like her to open her own stable. They take lessons from her, but they do not have the time or experience to help her run the business. Marielle suggests that three of her clients form a limited partnership of which she will be general partner and will work full-time to manage the business. The investors will provide the working capital and will own an interest in the business. The responsibilities and obligations of the respective parties are to be set out in a limited partnership agreement.

A limited partnership agreement requires a list of the rights and powers of the general partner, Marielle, versus the rights and powers of the limited partners, her friends. The accounting system is much more complex because the entire agreement is a meshing of two groups with different liabilities and financial commitments to the partnership.

Furthermore, the income or losses allocated to the limited partners are, by law, passive income. Horse owners and breeders are aware of a provision in the tax code that limits the deduction of losses from any business activity in which a person does not "materially participate," i.e., passive losses. Consequently, fewer people may be willing to invest in the highly risky business of horses without tax incentives; thus, the limited partnership is not as favorable an option as it was in the past.

A sample of a limited partnership agreement is not included here because persons contemplating limited partnerships should seek professional guidance.

SYNDICATIONS

Syndication is a relatively familiar term in the horse world, but the word is somewhat misleading. Under the tax law, a syndicate is not a separate way of doing business. Depending upon the particular arrangement and its activities, a syndicate created to breed, race, or show horses may be either a partnership or a joint ownership.

Although it is more desirable to treat a syndicate as a co-ownership of property, this is not always possible. Under the tax law, a partnership exists when two or more persons join together to carry on a business and share in the profits and losses. A partnership return is required, which adds time, expense, and complexity. The examples that follow will show the difference between two types of syndications.

Syndicate as Co-ownership

- Stallion syndicate in which breeding rights are reserved to the shareholders and NO breeding services are sold to the public by the syndicate.
- Joint ownership of a show horse as an investment.

Syndicate as Partnership

- Syndicate owns a stallion and sells breeding rights to non-syndicate members.
- Syndicate owns the broodmare(s) and sells the foals.
- Syndicate owns the racehorse(s) and shares in the purses.

In all forms of syndication, the investors share the expense and reduce their risks by allowing each investor to buy a share in one or more horses, or by ensuring breeding rights in a particular stallion. It is a form of group ownership, usually formed for a particular short-term purpose.

Because of the recent tax changes and because syndication agreements vary greatly, each carrying different tax benefits and liabilities, the investor must seek professional advice. Also, in addition to tax impact, investors may be subject to state and federal securities laws.

When a person is relatively uninformed and unskilled and then turns over his money to others relying on their professional or management skill to manage it, the transaction is called an investment security. Under federal law, selling unregistered securities is a criminal act, punishable by heavy fines or imprisonment or both. Preparing and filing a registration statement is a lengthy and expensive procedure, although where the offering is made to a limited number of people or involves relatively small amounts of money, there are exceptions to the registration requirement. The person selling interests, as well as the investor, must seek legal counsel before creating a limited partnership or other organization in which interests will be sold.

Example: Two friends wish to buy a show horse. One can't afford the cost of buying the horse alone. The second friend is not a serious rider but loves the thrill of seeing the horse they own in the show ring. They need a syndicate agreement that is a co-ownership. It sets forth the rights and obligations of each of them under a syndication agreement. Syndication agreements can run 150 pages alone, but the one that follows, with only two persons involved, has been kept very simple.

SYNDICATE AGREEMENT

AGREEMENT, made _____ (date), between the persons whose names and addresses are set out in the Schedule attached and who have subscribed for the number of units set forth opposite their names ("Owners").

RECITALS

The Owners desire to form a Syndicate to purchase the gelding Hope and Glory, Quarterhorse, foaled 1990 herein referred to as the "horse."

The Owners will pay the sum of $ 6,250.00 per unit. There shall be 10 units in this Syndicate. Nancy Rider, acting for this Syndicate, shall purchase the horse for the sum of $ 62,500.00 and will accept delivery of the horse.

Upon said purchase of the horse, the Syndicate shall be in existence for the ownership and management of the horse upon the following terms and conditions:

1. Ownership.

The ownership of the horse shall be 10 units, to be insured at a price of $ 6,250.00 per unit; each of the 10 units shall be on an equal basis with the others, and only a full unit shall have any rights.

2. Location.

The horse shall be stabled at Stallion Farm on Stableview Road, Bareback, New York 12345 subject to change by consensus, and shall be under the personal supervision of Nancy Rider , as Syndicate Manager.

3. Manager's Duties.

Subject to the approval of the Partner(s), the Syndicate Manager shall have full charge of and control over the management of the horse and of all training matters arising out of this enterprise, subject to the approval of the Owners. She shall keep accurate account of all expenses. She shall exercise her best judgment in all training decisions.

4. Transferability.

Units may be transferred subject to the terms of this Agreement, provided, however, that each Owner shall have the first refusal to purchase any unit or units that an Owner may desire to sell.

5. Expenses.

Each Owner shall pay his proper share of the expenses of the Syndicate, including organizational, legal, accounting, board, advertising, veterinary, etc., proportionate to the number of units which he holds. Bills will be sent out monthly and are payable within ten days.

6. Liability of Manager.

The Syndicate Manager shall not be personally liable for any act or omission committed by her except for willful misconduct or gross negligence.

7. Insurance.

The Syndicate Manager shall be responsible for insuring the horse. The expense of the insurance shall be shared by the Partners in accordance with this Agreement.

8. Accounting.

The Syndicate Manager shall furnish each Partner periodically with a statement showing the receipts and expenditures and such other information as she may deem pertinent.

9. Special Meetings.

A special meeting of the Partner(s) may be called by either Partner at any time of mutual convenience with reasonable notice.

10. Active Participation.

Notwithstanding Manager's duties, each Partner shall materially and substantially participate in the day-to-day decisions affecting and relating to this joint venture and all management decisions relating to said horse.

11. Notices.

All required notices shall be effective and binding if sent by prepaid registered mail, telegram, cable, or delivered in person to the address of the respective Owners set out in the Schedule attached. Such address changes shall hereafter be designated in writing to the Syndicate Manager, addressed to: Nancy Rider, Stableview Road, Bareback, New York 12345.

12. Miscellaneous.

This Agreement, when executed by the Owners, shall constitute the Agreement between the parties, and shall be binding upon the Owners, their heirs, and assigns.

13. Liability.

This Agreement shall not be deemed to create any relationship by reason of which any party might be held liable for the omission or commission of any other party, unless otherwise provided.

14. Termination.

This Syndicate terminates on the sale of the horse at which time the Syndicate Manager shall furnish each Partner with an accounting. All income and expenses shall be shared in accordance with the proportionate ownership of units.

15. (a) Governing Law.

This Agreement shall be construed in accordance with and shall be governed by the laws of the State of _____ .
Any legal action must be brought in the county/municipality of_____.

OR

(b) Arbitration.

The parties to this Agreement mutually agree that any and all disputes arising in connection with this Agreement shall be settled and determined by binding arbitration conducted in accordance with the then existing rules of the American Arbitration Association by one or more arbitrators appointed in accordance with said rules. Said arbitration shall take place in _____(municipality), _____ (state).

16. Entire Agreement.

This constitutes the entire Agreement between the parties. Any modifications or additions MUST be in writing and signed by all parties to this Agreement. No oral modifications or additions will be considered to be part of this Agreement unless reduced to writing and signed by all parties.

IN WITNESS WHEREOF, we have executed this Agreement the day and date first above written.

_____
Signature

_____
Address

_____
Units Purchased

_____
Signature

_____
Address

_____
Units Purchased

Discussion of Syndicate Form

The agreement begins with the date and a brief introduction. The section called "Recitals" states the purpose of the syndicate to purchase a show horse named Hope and Glory. The horse is described briefly.

1. Next, the financial terms are stated. The purchase price of the horse is broken into ten units, at $6,250 per unit. In this example, there are two members of the syndicate, so each member buys five units. The purpose of this agreement is to buy one horse with the selling price already set. The scope and purpose of the syndicate will determine the cost per unit.

2. The location sets the stabling arrangement for the horse under the auspices of the syndicate manager.

3. The manager is given full control of all horse-related decisions subject to the approval of the owner(s). In this case, the manager is one of the members of the syndicate, but in any event she is expected to make her best effort and to act in good faith.

4. If one of the owners wants to sell, the other owner has the first option to buy out her units.

5. Each owner pays his proportionate share of all expenses, and bills are payable on a prompt basis.

6. The liability section is important since the manager cannot be sued for any damage to the horse unless she purposely committed an act of misconduct endangering the horse.

7. The manager must maintain insurance on the horse. She could be liable for the loss of the horse under Clause 6 if she purposely allows the policy to lapse.

8. The expenses and income of the syndicate must be regularly documented and mailed to the other owner(s).

9. Either owner can call a special meeting at a time and place convenient to both.

10. Each owner pledges to contribute substantial time to the daily business decisions. This section can be omitted, since the manager may realistically be responsible for most of the operation. The other owner here anticipated losses and wanted to provide for active participation under the tax law. The words alone will not ensure the tax outcome under the interpretation of the Internal Revenue Service. (See "Rules on Business Participation" under Partnership.)

11. All notices of meetings or other correspondence are binding if sent by registered mail, cabled, or hand delivered. Any address changes must be sent to the manager in writing.

12. The agreement represents all the terms. No one can complain later that there were oral additions to the writing and it is binding on any future parties with an interest in the syndicate.

13. Neither party is liable to the other for something not stated within this agreement.

14. The syndicate is no longer in existence once the horse is sold. At the point of the sale, the proceeds are split in proportion to the ownership interest.

15. Under "Governing Law" the controlling state is named and the venue for any litigation. Or an "Arbitration" clause may be selected, which elects that in the event of a dispute, the parties will go to Arbitration rather than to court.

Finally, the agreement is signed with the addresses and units purchased stated. This agreement does not take into account the complexity of appraising units or the method of calculating each owner's account. Any syndicate with more members or greater complexity would require professional advice, but a blank copy of this form is included as a model in the appendix.

CORPORATION

In the regular corporation, the skill and managerial expertise are provided by the paid employees of the corporation who may or may not own any stock. This is a more expensive and complicated way of doing business. Unlike proprietorships and partnerships, the corporation itself is a taxpaying entity; the corporation pays taxes on its profits. When profits are distributed to shareholders, the shareholders pay an additional tax based on their individual tax bracket. The corporate stockholders, like the limited partners, can be held liable for no more than their original investment; there is no personal liability for business losses, debts, negligence, and other similar items. At its most sophisticated levels, stocks of horse-racing farms have been sold publicly and the organization is regulated by securities laws.

To incorporate, an individual must file the Articles of Incorporation with the state, paying the necessary fees. At this point, the individuals involved in organizing the corporation usually transfer money or property to the newly formed corporation in exchange for stock of the corporation. The corporation begins business for tax purposes when it starts the activities for which it was organized. See sample form page 23.

It should be noted that although a corporate form generally protects the stockholders from personal liability, under certain circumstances the "corporate veil" can be pierced and the stockholders held personally liable. This can occur when the corporation is under-capitalized or when the corporation is a mere shell and being used as the "alter ego" of an individual stockholder.

THE ARTICLES OF INCORPORATION

FIRST: I,_____ , whose post office address is_____ _____ , being at least eighteen (18) years of age, hereby forms a corporation under and by virtue of the General Laws of the State of_____ .

SECOND: The name of the corporation (hereinafter referred to as the "Corporation") is_____ _____ .

THIRD: The purposes for which the Corporation is formed are:
    (1) To conduct a riding stable including a lesson program, to maintain a sales barn, and to maintain a string of show horses for outside owners.
    (2) To do anything permitted by the appropriate laws of the state.

FOURTH: The post office address of the principal office of the Corporation in this state is_____ _____ . The name and post office address of the Resident Agent of the Corporation are _____ _____ . Said Resident Agent resides in this state.

FIFTH: The total number of shares of capital stock that the Corporation has authority to issue is_____ _____ shares of common stock, without par value.

SIXTH: The number of Directors of the Corporation shall be increased or decreased pursuant to the By-Laws of the Corporation, but shall not be fewer than three unless:
    (1) there is no stock held but then no fewer than one; or
    (2) if no fewer than the number of stockholders.

SEVENTH: The names of the directors who shall act until the first meeting are _____ _____ .

EIGHTH: The following provisions define, limit, and regulate the powers of the Corporation, the directors, and stockholders:
    (1) The Board of Directors of the Corporation may issue stock.
    (2) The Board of Directors may classify or reclassify unissued stock.
    (3) The Corporation may amend its Charter to alter contract rights of any outstanding stock.
    (4) [Any other specific right can be enumerated here.]
    Any enumeration of rights is not meant to limit any powers conferred upon the Board of Directors under state statute now in force or in force in the future.

NINTH: Unless the Board of Directors states otherwise, no shareholder has special rights to buy, convert, or in any other way to acquire stocks.

    I sign these Articles of Incorporation this_____day of _____(month), _____ (year).

_____
Signature

Discussion of the Articles of Incorporation

The Articles that must be on file with the state are straightforward.

1. Name(s) of the person(s) who are forming the corporation with address and home state.

2. The name of the corporation.

3. The purpose of the corporation is set out in general terms.

4. The person who will be the resident agent is named for mailing purposes and is the contact within the state; e.g., to whom all paperwork is sent.

5. The total number of shares is stated. Usually, these shares are not given any set (or par) value.

6. The number of directors is established.

7. The directors for the first meeting are named.

8. The rights and limitations of the powers of the Board of Directors are listed. Usually, these are very broad because this group is the executive body of the corporation.

9. No shareholder is to receive special rights to acquire additional stock over and above the other shareholders.

Finally, the Articles are signed by the person(s) forming the corporation. Filing these Articles is a formality that establishes the Corporation as a tax-paying entity with its own separate identity.

S CORPORATION

The S Corporation provides the advantages of limited liability without problems of double taxation. It is a special type of corporation designed for the small business owner, and the same general procedures must be followed for creating the S Corporation as are described for the corporation. In general, the S Corporation may have no more than thirty-five shareholders and must file an election with the Internal Revenue Service within seventy-five days of doing business. Unlike the regular corporation, the income and losses pass through directly to the shareholders as they would in a partnership and are reported on their personal income tax returns. The active or passive nature of the income depends on each individual shareholder's involvement. The reasons for electing to form a Subchapter S Corporation is to obtain the advantages of incorporation, but, at the same time, to have the tax advantages of a partnership. When the business shows losses in the early years, a Subchapter S Corporation can pass those losses through to the shareholders to be deducted against their income. If the business becomes profitable, the income of the corporation is not taxed both to the business and then to the individual.

The major disadvantage to setting up either an S Corporation or a regular corporation is the amount of effort and cost involved. Legal assistance is advised and the costs for incorporation with the organizational basics listed vary depending on your location. However, a person can shop around for reasonable fees. Any attorney hired, however, should have experience in this area, because there can be major tax consequences as a result of a decision to form a corporation.

SUMMARY

This chapter has attempted to focus on key characteristics of certain types of businesses and the types of contracts associated with them. It is impossible to generalize about the form best suited for a particular horse business because it depends on the exact circumstances of the business and the people involved. In general, however, the simpler the form used, the lower will be legal and accounting expenses. For instance, there are adverse tax consequences on the transfer of property from a corporation to a shareholder, and the termination of either kind of corporation can be expensive. **A tax advisor is needed to analyze the advantages and disadvantages.** The following list summarizes the main points of each way of doing business:

Sole Proprietorship

- one person only
- higher individual tax rates
- direct use of losses against personal income
- business can terminate at any time
- personal liability in the event of a lawsuit
- material participation rules unlikely to limit use of losses
- least expensive to set up and maintain
- easiest, simplest form

Partnership

- more than one person
- income taxed at individual rate only
- direct use of losses against personal income
- distribution of property or cash is not taxed
- easily liquidated
- personal liability for partners in the event of a lawsuit
- material participation rules unlikely to limit use of losses
- relatively simple form

Limited Partnership

- less complex than a corporation
- more than one person involved, with general partner(s) who run the business and limited partner(s) who invest
- income taxed at individual rate only
- distributions of property or cash are not taxed
- limited partners partially sheltered from personal liability
- material participation rules define losses as passive for all limited partners
- more complex form

Corporation

- taxed at two levels: corporate and individual
- any distribution of property or cash to shareholders is taxed
- some income accumulated at corporate level is not distributed
- personal liability of shareholders against debt, negligence, and other obligations of the business is limited
- lower tax rates for the corporation
- transferable units for estate-planning purposes
- expensive to establish and maintain
- losses may be used to offset other corporate profits
- complex form

S Corporation

- income must be distributed to shareholders
- pass through of losses and income taxed at individual level
- must file an election with IRS within seventy-five days
- easier to get appreciated property out of the corporation
- limited personal liability (same as corporation)
- individual tax rates apply
- provides transferable unit for estate-planning purposes
- expensive to establish and maintain
- complex form

4

Appraisal

An appraisal is a statement establishing a horse's value if the horse were to be sold in the open market. A person who is considered an expert in the field of buying and selling horses makes an educated opinion on the worth of a horse.

Example: A horse owner chooses to donate a horse to a charitable institution that is a nonprofit organization registered with the Internal Revenue Service. The owner wishes to receive tax credit for making a charitable donation, and, therefore, needs to know the value of the horse. (The tax consequences are discussed in *Tax Planning and Preparation for Horse Owners,* Breakthrough Publications, updated annually.)

A qualified stable owner or someone who regularly buys and sells horses, for example, may be asked to make such an appraisal. A copy of the appraisal will be given to the organization when the horse is donated and will be attached to the owner's tax return. A general idea of the form is helpful.

In the sample appraisal that follows, the horse was a relatively young horse that had not been shown or hunted. The appraiser was not previously familiar with this horse but was asked by the college to conduct an appraisal for a prospective donor.

APPRAISAL OF A YOUNG HORSE NEVER SHOWN

I am qualified to appraise the value of a horse in today's market. I have been buying and selling show hunters for the last twenty-five years and am considered an expert in the field.

I have personally evaluated the horse described as follows within the last ___Ten___ (__10__) days:

Name: Cold Sassy Tree

Age: 7 years

Breed: Appaloosa/Thoroughbred cross

Sex: Gelding

Size: 16 h 2"

This horse is owned by __John Q. Horseman__ residing at __29 Stableview Road, Bareback, New York__ and said horse is being donated to __Appaloosa College of Lexington, Kentucky__. Based on the soundness, size, disposition, and athletic ability of this horse, I would set the fair market value at __Nine Thousand Five Hundred Dollars__ ($__9,500.00__). This price is fair and reasonable given the market and demand for horses of this type.

This appraisal price is an objective estimate to the best of my ability and knowledge on this _____ day of _____ (month), _____ (year).

_____
Signature of Appraiser

Discussion

In the first paragraph, the appraiser establishes her credentials by stating the number of years she has been in the business and in what capacity. Next, the horse is described and the owner is identified with an address. Finally and most importantly, the appraiser states the basis of the appraisal price and sets an exact figure to the best of her knowledge. Obviously, the worth of a horse is highly subjective and speculative, but the appraiser may be subject to prosecution if she purposely misstates the value of the horse. Then she signs and dates the document.

Paragraph 1: State your credentials as an expert in the horse business for the type of horse being appraised.

Paragraphs 2 and 3: State the name and address of the donor, the place of donation if known, and a full description of the horse.

Describe the basis of the appraisal and the monetary fair-market value of the horse to the best of your knowledge.

The basis of the appraisal is a recent first-hand observation of the horse, considering external factors, such a show record, winnings, or breeding potential in today's market. As real estate appraisers do with houses, you might use comparable horses and their selling prices as an evaluative tool.

Owners will often tell the appraiser what they paid for the horse or the additional amounts they have invested in the horse. Often these figures are not very reliable guidelines in the appraisal process because commonly a horse is not worth its purchase price (another sad reality of the horse business).

Finally, the form is dated and signed.

5

Bill of Sale

A Bill of Sale is a document signed by the seller stating that he or she received a certain amount of money in exchange for a horse sold to the buyer named. The Bill of Sale serves as proof of ownership for the buyer and provides a statement that the seller has been paid in full. If a horse is sold at a profit, there is a potential tax liability. On audit, the Internal Revenue Service may ask to see the Bill of Sale.

When purchasing a horse, the buyer should always get a Bill of Sale warranting ownership and stating the seller's address. All official registration should be transferred **at the time of the sale**, and in that way you avoid the sad case of the person who buys a Thoroughbred, but never receives the papers or a Bill of Sale. He or she may be told "it is in the mail," and eight months later the buyer is contacted by the real owner who is not the person who sold the horse. The real owner sues the buyer for the return of the horse. After six more months, the buyer loses the horse to the owner, but is reimbursed for the board bills. The buyer must track down the seller and enforce a judgment for the purchase price against the fraudulent seller who has no job and no money. Buyer suffers heart-break and the loss of the purchase price.

Example: Judy has finally talked her parents into buying her a horse. They find a suitable horse. Dad writes a check for one thousand dollars ($1,000) to Jane Q. Rider and Judy rides the horse home. He receives the following bill of sale (page 32).

Discussion

This is a simple and direct Bill of Sale. "I," the person selling, followed by an address, states how much money was paid and by whom and who lives where. Next, the horse is described. The seller promises he is the owner and had the right to sell and will defend against any claims to the contrary. The form is then executed with a signature and dated.

A more complex Bill of Sale may be necessary if the horse is very expensive and the owner is making additional warranties as to the horse's breeding record, show winnings, or suitability for a particular purpose, or, for the case where a mare is sold in foal to a particular stallion, with a breeding certificate attached. (See Chapter 9, Purchase Agreement.)

SAMPLE

BILL OF SALE

I, ___Jane Q. Rider___ , residing at ___29 Stableview Road,___ ___Bareback, Maryland___ , in consideration of ___One Thousand___ ___Dollars ($1,000)___ , hereby paid to me by ___John Q. Horseman___ , residing at ___Saddle Lane, Meadow, MD___ , sell to ___John Q. Horseman___ the following described horse:

Name:	Sassy
Age:	8 years
Color:	Chestnut
Breed:	Quarter Horse (no papers)
Sex:	Mare
Size:	15 h 2"

I hereby covenant that I am the lawful owner of the horse; that I have the right to sell the horse; and that I will warrant and defend said horse against lawful claims and demands of all persons.

Executed this ___4th___ day of ___July___ , _____(date), under the laws of the State of ___Maryland___ .

_____
Signature of Seller

6

Consignment Agreement
for Sale of Horse
and
Limited Power of Attorney

In a consignment agreement an owner entrusts his horse to another person whose job is to sell the horse. Thus, instead of finding a buyer himself, the seller signs a contract with a middleman who handles the sale. In most consignment agreements the owner sends the horse to the barn of the salesperson, the consignment stable.

The person who takes the horse on consignment is acting as an agent for the owner. He or she is given the authority to sign a bill of sale and collect money for the owner through a second agreement, called a limited power of attorney. It is called a limited power of attorney because the power of the agent to act in place of the owner is limited to this horse transaction and to the specific terms of this agreement.

Example: Jane Rider owns a big quarter horse mare, but the horse is not suitable for her. She decides to send the horse to a local professional to be sold. She is familiar with the excellent quality of this sales stable and has personally inspected the stables and turnout facilities. She has also spoken with satisfied customers who have sold their horses through this agent.

She paid five thousand dollars ($5,000) for the mare and wants to sell her for that. She knows the horse is a hard keeper and requires special feeding. The mare is temperamental, and Jane does not want her transferred to other barns before money changes hands. She has heard that some horses have been sold while under medication unbeknown to the buyer. She wants to address all these concerns in the contract.

Jane, the consignor, should prepare a consignment agreement authorizing the consignee to act as an agent in this sale. She also needs to prepare a power of attorney agreement attached as a separate form.

CONSIGNMENT AGREEMENT

THIS AGREEMENT is made between _____Jane Rider_____, the "Consignor," residing at _____Horsetown, New York_____, and_____John Horseman_____, the "Consignee," residing at _____Westriver, New York_____.

1. Description.

The Consignor owns a horse described in this section below:

(a) Name: Saddle Deck

(b) Age: 10 years

(c) Breed: Quarter horse

(d) Sex: Mare

(e) Size: 16 hands

(f) Markings and color: Chestnut, star and stripe
White sock, right front

2. Purpose.

The Consignee is in the business of buying and selling horses as an agent. the Consignor desires to sell said horse. Consignee agrees to make his best effort to sell said horse on behalf of the Consignor.

3. Warranties.

The Consignee accepts said horse into his sales barn under the following terms:

(a) The minimum selling price for the horse is Five Thousand ($5,000.00) Dollars unless changed in writing by the Consignor before a sale.

(b) The horse will not be released on trial without Consignor's written consent.

(c) The horse will not be used for lesson, show, or lease purposes while under this consignment agreement without Consignor's written consent.

(d) The Consignor will not ride the horse while under this Agreement.

4. Board.

In consideration of _$550.00_ per horse per month paid by Consignor in advance on the first day of each month, the Consignee agrees to board said horse until sold or this Agreement is terminated.

5. Commission.

At the sale of said horse, the Consignee shall receive a commission of _10_% on all funds received. The Consignor shall receive the balance of all funds on the sale of said horse within 10 days. The Consignee shall charge _1/2_ % late fee per month on any late payment.

6. Care of Horse.

(a) The Consignee agrees to provide normal and reasonable care to maintain the health and well-being of said horse. This care includes (i)_____daily grooming_____,
(ii)_____blanketing when necessary_____, and (iii)_____daily individual_____ turnout for brief periods_____.

(b) Routine veterinary and farrier care are authorized with direct billing. Any extraordinary care requires the consent of the Consignor unless on an emergency basis.

(c) The following feed and supplements shall be fed daily:

Hay: 5 large flakes   2 times daily
Grain: 6 lbs.   2 times daily
Daily supplements:
          Biotin
          Mirra Coat
          Electrolytes

(d) Exercise
Said horse shall be ridden or lunged by Consignee or a competent rider employed by Consignee at least _____four_____ days a week.

The Consignee will show the horse to potential buyers under the following terms.

(1) Said horse does not leave the grounds of the Consignee.

(2) The horse is not ridden by potential buyers more than twice a day.

(3) The horse is not medicated for any exercise or presentation to buyers.

7. Retention of Title and Assumption of Risk at Sale.

Consignor retains title to horse. The title passes from Consignor to Buyer, and Buyer may take possession only upon transfer of full consideration to Consignee. Consignor retains risk of loss until title and possession pass to Buyer on the above conditions. Buyer assumes all risk and costs at the point of said transfer and prior to the horse's release from Consignee's premises.

None of the above terms are subject to change without explicit written agreement by the Consignor.

8. Lien.

Consignee agrees to keep horse free and clear of all liens and encumbrances.

9. Attorney's Fees.

This Agreement is terminated upon a breach of any material term, and the wronged party has the right to collect all reasonable fees and costs from the breaching party.

10. Termination.

Either party may cancel this agreement prior to sale on _____five_____ days written notice and final accounting thereto.

11. (a) Governing Law.

This Agreement shall be construed in accordance with and shall be governed by the laws of the State of New York_____. Any legal action must be brought in the county/municipality of Horsetown_____.

OR

(b) Arbitration.

The parties to this Agreement mutually agree that any and all disputes arising in connection with this Agreement shall be settled and determined by binding arbitration conducted in accordance with the then existing rules of the American Arbitration Association by one or more arbitrators appointed in accordance with said rules. Said arbitration shall take place in_____Horsetown_____ (municipality), __New York_____ (state).

12. Entire Agreement.

This constitutes the entire Agreement between the parties. Any modifications or additions MUST be in writing and signed by all parties to this Agreement. No oral modifications or additions will be considered to be part of this Agreement unless reduced to writing and signed by all parties.

_____   _____
Date   Signature of Consignor

_____   _____
Date   Signature of Consignee

Discussion of Consignment Agreement

Once the consignor, Jane, is personally satisfied with this sales barn, she is the one to provide the agreement.

1. In the first section, both parties are named with addresses given, and the horse is described. If a horse has any other distinguishing features, these might be included.

2. The purpose of the agreement is stated. The seller, Jane, is the consignor and she is sending her horse to a sales agent, the consignee, who will make his best efforts to sell her horse.

3. **(a)** This is the minimum price the owner is willing to accept for the horse. (They may agree to ask more at first.) This term is very important. Jane may reduce this figure in writing or, under the more optimistic circumstances, raise it, but only if a sale has not been consummated.

   (b) In the following paragraphs, there are blank spaces for any other specific terms required by either party:
   Here Jane does not want this horse to be moved to another barn for a trial period before the sale (a requisite of many buyers). She may have to change this provision later.

   (c) The horse is not available for purposes other than sale, e.g., lessons, show, or lease. The owner should recognize that some sales barns also function as lesson stables where the board is reduced if the horse is used in lessons. Sometimes these lessons can lead to a sale to a rider in the barn. Showing does give the horse exposure and leasing reduces costs. On the other hand, Jane must weigh the advantages against the inherent risks of injury. If she does allow the horse to be used in lessons, anyone riding the horse must have a liability release on file with the agent or consignee. Whichever route is chosen, the terms must be explicitly stated.

   (d) The last term is included by the consignee. He may find that owners show up at inopportune times to ride their horses when he has clients lined up. Some owners are poor riders who are detriments to the sale of their own horses. Whatever the agent's policy, the rules must be clarified.

4. The cost of board is set. The horse continues to eat until sold. The consignee rarely fronts the costs until the time of sale.

5. The amount of commission on the sales price is established. Some agents set a sales price over and above the owner's price and collect the difference as profit. This practice can lead to inflated sales prices if the owner does not understand that this will be the case. Whatever the practice, the consignor needs to get this in writing.

The consignor should receive the sales money promptly with a late charge as penalty.

6. The care of the horse is clarified.

It is important to inspect the facility before entrusting the horse to the sales agent or anyone connected with the barn.

   (a) Once satisfied with the place, Jane may still specify the daily care. This section protects the agent also, because he can stipulate what care is included in his base price. Because the consignor is often not at the stable on a regular basis, grooming and daily care are necessary for sales purposes.

   (b) Routine veterinary and farrier care are provided with direct billing. Emergency care is authorized until the owner can be notified.

(c) Feeding schedules and supplements are of assistance to the consignee who, like the owner, wants the horse well-maintained. There may be additional fees in this section to cover the supplements or special feeding.

(d) Exercise can be specified as to number of times per week or can be left open. The rider is also generally designated as an employee of the barn.

7. The risk of the horse's death or injury passes to the buyer when the horse is still at the consignee's barn and once the buyer has paid in full and has received the relevant paperwork. This may include Thoroughbred papers, a bill of sale, or any other formal registration. The buyer assumes all costs at this point and arranges for delivery of the horse. If the horse dies before she leaves the consignee's barn, the buyer still owns the horse and is not entitled to a refund.

It is possible to sell on an installment basis, but the owner/consignor must consent in writing. Secondly, the consignee may take his entire commission at the time of the sale. These details require additional terms. (See Chapter 8 and the Promissory Note form.)

8. Even the most established stables have been known to declare bankruptcy. The horses owned by the consignee become the property of the bank or creditors and may be sold at auction. This section provides that the consigned horse is kept free and clear of any financial obligations of the consignee. The ownership should *never* be signed over to the consignee, even when there is an explicit understanding that the agent is only "pretending" to be the owner.

9. If either party does not abide by the agreement, the other person may terminate the agreement. If the disagreement cannot be resolved, the person who broke the agreement is responsible for reasonable attorney's fees and court costs.

10. "Termination" allows Jane to change her mind about selling, or she may move the horse after giving five days notice. Sometimes an agent recognizes that he can't sell the horse and recommends a different location for the horse. They both have this flexibility.

11. Under "Governing Law," the controlling state is named. Different states have different laws. A consignee might live in New Jersey but ride in Connecticut. The consignee's residence may be New York. The county or municipality where any legal action would be brought is named. Instead of using the Governing Law clause, you may use the "Arbitration" clause, because taking a party to court is very expensive and time consuming. Arbitration is not cheap, or easy, or speedy either, but it is still quicker and easier than litigation.

Finally, the agreement is signed and dated. Remember, there must be signatures or no agreement exists.

SAMPLE

LIMITED POWER OF ATTORNEY

I, _____ Jane Rider _____, of _____ Horsetown, New York _____, do hereby execute this Limited Power of Attorney with the intention that the attorney-in-fact hereinafter named shall be able to act in my place for the purposes set forth herein.

Section 1. Designation of Attorney.

I constitute and appoint_____ John _____ Horseman _____ to be my attorney-in-fact to act for me, in my name, and in my place.

Section 2. Effective Date of Power of Attorney.

2.01 This Limited Power of Attorney shall be effective as of the date of its execution by me, and shall remain effective unless same revoked by me, until midnight on_____ .

2.02 This Limited Power of Attorney shall not be affected by my disability, it being my specific intention that my attorney-in-fact shall continue to act as such even though I may not be competent to ratify the actions of my attorney-in-fact.

Section 3. Powers.

3.01 My attorney-in-fact shall have all of the powers, discretions, elections, and authorities granted by statute, common law, and under any rule of court necessary to sell my__ 10-__ year-old, 16 hand Quarter horse mare named "Saddle Deck" for a price of at least $5,000.00 __ . In addition thereto, and not in limitation thereof, my attorney-in-fact shall also have the power set forth below.

3.02 My attorney-in-fact may collect and receive, with or without the institution of suit or other legal process, all debts, monies, objects,

interest, and demands due to me pursuant to the aforementioned sale.

3.03 My attorney-in-fact may endorse my name for deposit into a savings, checking, or money-market account of mine with respect to sums payable to me pursuant to the aforementioned sale.

3.04 My attorney-in-fact may execute, seal, acknowledge, and deliver any documents necessary, advisable, or expedient with respect to the aforementioned sale.

Section 4. Ratification.

4.01 I hereby ratify, allow, acknowledge, and hold firm and valid all acts heretofore or hereafter taken by my attorney-in-fact by virtue of these presents in connection with the aforementioned contract.

AS WITNESS my hand and seal this _____ day of _____(month), _____(year).

WITNESS:

_____

_____

_____

Jane Rider   (SEAL)

Discussion of Limited Power of Attorney

The agent, here John Horseman, needs a power of attorney from Jane to sell the horse. Once this form is executed, he will be acting as an authorized agent, a kind of owner-replacement, just for the purpose of this sale.

1.   First, the consignor, Jane, is named with her address and her intent to authorize John Horseman as her agent.

2.   She sets the term of the agreement, unless revoked sooner. She also provides for his on-going authority over the contract in the event she suffers a disability, i.e., coma, or is declared mentally incompetent by the court.

3.   Thirdly, she confers all powers necessary to sell the horse as named and described for the agreed-upon price. The agent may collect all fees due and handle all financial aspects of the sale, including deposits at the bank.
   If any papers must be signed, he may write his signature as agent for the owner and deliver all necessary documents.

4.   Finally, Jane states that she will stand behind all acts of the agent within the scope of this agreement. Then she dates and signs with a person witnessing the signature. The word "seal" is a formality.

This power of attorney will be executed at the time of the Consignment Agreement.

7

Agreement for the Sale of Unborn Foal

Sometimes a buyer wishes to lock up the purchase of the offspring of the breeding of a particularly desirable stallion and mare. An agreement for the sale of an unborn foal allows the buyer to prepurchase the foal prior to its actual birth, upon the terms and conditions mutually agreed to by the buyer and seller and as set forth in the agreement, including the predetermined and agreed-upon purchase price.

Since this type of contract is usually executed well in advance of the birth of the foal in question, the contract is considered "executory" in nature, which means that the contract has yet to be carried out, or is dependent upon some further condition or event. In the case of a contract for the sale of an unborn foal, of course, the contract can only be enforced upon the birth of a live and healthy foal; therefore, the parties should agree upon the definition of what constitutes a live and healthy foal. This definition, once agreed upon, should then be set forth in the body of the agreement itself.

In the sample agreement, the definition of a live and healthy foal is one who is born alive and lives for ninety-six hours. The agreement also states that the foal must be pronounced as healthy and free of defects by a veterinarian within this ninety-six-hour period. Definitions may vary, from a live foal standing and nursing to alive for thirty-six hours, and so on.

SAMPLE

AGREEMENT FOR SALE OF UNBORN FOAL

THIS IS AN AGREEMENT BETWEEN _____Tom and Mary Jones_____, hereinafter referred to as "Buyer" and _____Shannon Smith_____ , hereinafter referred to as "Seller," who is the sole owner of the mare,_____"Hearts on Fire"_____, hereinafter referred to as "mare."

A foal is due to be born to said mare on or about the month of _____April 1997_____ by _____George's Golden Boy, Reg. No. 123456_____ [stallion's name and I.D.].

In consideration of the promises and of the recitals set forth herein by Buyer and Seller, Buyer hereby agrees to buy and Seller hereby agrees to sell the unborn foal upon the following terms and conditions:

1. Location, Cost of Care and Maintenance, Title.

(a) Seller will, according to the terms of this Agreement, board the mare and the foal at no cost to Buyer until such time as the foal is weaned (in no event earlier than five months after foal's birth) and possession of the foal is transferred to Buyer. The Buyer is responsible for all veterinary expenses for foal after _____first 96 hours of life_____.

(b) Seller expressly promises and agrees that neither Seller nor anyone acting on Seller's behalf shall remove mare or her foal from _____Windward Farms, 999 Main Street, Horseback, NY_____unless and until both Buyer and Seller have given express written consent to the move.

(c) In which case, Seller shall give Buyer thirty (30) days written notice of any such proposed change of location during which time Buyer shall make all appropriate filings or recordings necessary to fully protect Buyer's interest in the foal; however, in no event shall the mare or foal be located outside of the United States of America or within any jurisdiction within the United States of America that has not adopted the Uniform Commercial Code.

(d) Seller does and shall retain full title to the mare; however, so long as the foal is in utero, Seller recognizes Buyer's interest in said foal and agrees not to transfer, lease, sell or in any way hypothecate Seller's interest in said mare. Seller further agrees that until the foal has been weaned, Seller shall not sell or in any way transfer or hypothecate Seller's interest in the mare to any other person.

(e) The term of this Sale Agreement as to the mare and foal shall begin on the date set forth herein and shall terminate when all conditions have been fulfilled and physical possession of the foal is given to Buyer.

(f) Seller agrees to provide and maintain a proper environment for the mare and foal with all stabling, turnout area, appropriate feed, constant supply of fresh water, veterinary care, and all other reasonable and necessary goods and services for the mare and foal until such time as the foal has been weaned and physical possession of the foal has been given to the Buyer.

2. Purchase Price.

Buyer agrees to pay to Seller _____ten thousand ($10,000)_____Dollars as follows:

(a) Upon the signing of this Agreement, Buyer tenders the amount of _____five thousand ($5,000)_____Dollars, the receipt and sufficiency whereof is hereby acknowledged by Seller.

(b) On or before _____(date), Buyer shall deposit in an escrow fund (such as an attorney's trust account) the amount which is the balance of the purchase price agreed upon.

(c) The above-referenced balance shall be paid out of the trust account to Seller upon the fulfillment of the following terms and conditions:

(i) Mare foals out.

(ii) The foal is pronounced live, healthy, and insurable by a doctor of veterinary medicine within 96 hours of foaling and a certificate of good health shall be signed and delivered to Buyer or Buyer's attorney by a doctor of veterinary medicine.

(iii) Buyer has received written confirmation of full all risk mortality and accident insurance on said foal in the full amount of the purchase price and the beneficiary of the insurance shall be Buyer herein and shall insure his interest in the foal for the full purchase amount; and the statement for the premium of said insurance policy shall be sent to Buyer for payment.

3. Conditions Precedent.

Buyer's obligations to deliver the balance of the purchase price shall be subject to the satisfaction of the following conditions precedent.

(a) Mare shall give birth to a live foal by George's Golden Boy (Name of Stallion) on or about _____ (date), but in no event before _____ (date).

(b) Said foal shall remain alive and in good health for at least ninety-six (96) hours, be sound and be both insurable and, in fact, insured for the full purchase price against all risks, naming Buyer as beneficiary.

(c) Said foal shall have no white markings above knee (state here any objectional markings peculiar to particular breed, but this condition precedent may be waived by Buyer at Buyer's sole discretion).

(d) The mare, Heart's on Fire (Name of Mare), shall be taken to 1245 Jefferson Street, Horseback, NY and shall remain at said location until the foal is weaned.

OR

Shall remain at Windward Farms, 999 Main Street, Horseback, NY until the foal is weaned.

(f) All documents which are required by the American Quarter Horse Registry to effect transfer of the foal from Seller to Buyer have been executed by Seller and delivered to Buyer or Buyer's attorney. It is understood that should the American Quarter Horse Registry or any other entity or body require any other forms or certificates signed by Seller, Seller shall, within five (5) days of receipt, properly complete and execute and return all documents sent to Seller by Buyer.

(g) The unborn foal has not in any way been sold to or hypothecated to anyone other than Buyer herein.

(h) This Agreement and all other documents to be executed by Seller have been duly authorized, executed, and delivered by Seller and constitute valid, legal, and binding agreements enforceable in accordance with their terms.

(i) The entering into and performance of this Agreement and the documents to be executed by Seller will not violate any judgment, order, law, or regulation applicable to Seller or result in any breach or constitute a default under, or result in the creation of any lien, charge, security interest, or other encumbrance upon a foal pursuant to any indenture, mortgage, deed of trust, bank loan or credit arrangement, or other instrument to which Seller is a party or by which it or its assets may be bound.

(j) There are no suits or proceedings pending, or to the knowledge of Seller, threatened in any court or before any regulatory commission, board, or other governmental authority against or affecting Seller, which will have a materially adverse effect on the ability of Seller to fulfill his obligations under this Sale Agreement.

(k) There exists no defect or impediment on the registration of the mare with the___American Quarter Horse Registry___, and the___American Quarter Horse Registry___ will issue a certificate for the foal when born, showing that its sire is___George's Golden Boy___ and its dam is___Heart's on Fire___, and that foal is a duly qualified and registered ___American Quarter Horse___foal.

[___Seller___/___Buyer___] will pay registration fees.

4. Taxes.

Seller agrees to pay and to indemnify and hold Buyer harmless from all license and registration fees and all taxes, including, without limitation, income, franchise, sales, use, personal property stamp, or other taxes, levies and post duties, charges, or withholdings of any nature, together with any penalties, fines, or interest thereon, imposed against Seller by any federal, state, or local government or a taxing authority with respect to the purchase, ownership, delivery, possession, use, or transfer with respect to the foal. All amounts payable by Seller pursuant to this section shall be payable to the extent not theretofore paid on written demand of Buyer.

5. Identification of Buyer.

Seller will, from the date of the signing of these documents to the date that physical possession of the foal is delivered to the Buyer, clearly identify by appropriate markings and/or in any conversations that the foal is owned by Buyer herein and Seller will expressly advise anyone who inquires or indicates any interest in either mare or the foal that Seller no longer has any interest in the foal and the fact the foal is owned by Buyer.

6. Notice.

Any notice required or permitted to be given by either party hereto shall be deemed to have been given when deposited in the United States certified mail, postage prepaid, and addressed to the other party at the address where indicated on the last page of this Agreement, or addressed to either part at such other address as such party shall hereafter furnish to the other party in writing.

7. Assignment.

Neither party shall assign this Agreement or their interest thereunder without the prior consent of the other party.

8. Termination by Buyer.

In the event that any obligation of the Seller has not been met or if any condition precedent set forth above has not been fulfilled, Buyer shall have the right to terminate this Agreement. Should Seller fail to do so upon demand from Buyer, Seller agrees to pay all costs and reasonable attorney's fees that Buyer may incur to collect said monies from Seller.

9. Default.

In case of default by the Seller, it is expressly agreed that Buyer may either revoke this Agreement and demand an immediate refund of all monies paid plus interest at the rate of___10%___per annum, or sue for specific performance and demand strict compliance by Seller with the terms of this Agreement, or any combination of the above and/or together with any and all remedies allowed by law. It is specifically agreed by Seller that should Seller default, whatever remedy or combination of remedies pursued by Buyer, Seller will pay as additional damages all costs, expenses, and reasonable attorney's fees incurred by Buyer in enforcing his rights hereunder.

Should Buyer default, it is agreed by both parties that Seller may retain any deposit monies tendered by the Buyer. The Seller must try to mitigate his or her damages by offering the unborn foal to other sellers. However, in the event that Seller is unable to secure another buyer at the same or greater price than the price originally agreed upon by the parties, the Buyer is responsible for the difference between the contract price and the actual sales price plus any actual or consequential damages incurred by the Seller.

10. (a) Governing Law.

This Agreement shall be construed in accordance with and shall be governed by the laws of the State of __New York__. Any legal action must be brought in the county/municipality of __Horseback, NY__.

OR

(b) Arbitration.

The parties to this Agreement mutually agree that any and all disputes arising in connection with this Agreement shall be settled and determined by binding arbitration conducted in accordance with the then existing rules of the American Arbitration Association by one or more arbitrators appointed in accordance with said rules. Said arbitration shall take place in __Horseback__ (municipality) __New York__ (state).

11. Liquidated Damages.

In the event of Seller's default in any of the provisions hereunder, it is agreed by the parties that Buyer's damages could vary widely and would be very difficult to ascertain. Therefore, the Buyer and Seller agree that should Seller default, Buyer has the option of demanding the sum of __twelve thousand ($12,000)__ Dollars from Seller as liquidated damages for any of Buyer's claims hereunder. This option shall be of no force and effect unless and until Buyer specifically elects in writing to pursue this remedy. This provision is not provided as a penalty and it is specifically agreed that should this remedy be selected by Buyer and suit brought to enforce the terms contained herein, that Seller, in addition to __twelve thousand ($12,000)__ Dollars of liquidated damages, will also pay all costs, expenses, and reasonable attorney's fees incurred by Buyer in enforcing this provision.

12. Entire Agreement.

This constitutes the entire Agreement between the parties. Any modifications or additions MUST be in writing and signed by all parties to this Agreement. No oral modifications or additions will be considered to be part of this Agreement unless reduced to writing and signed by all parties.

Dated: _____

Seller: Shannon Smith

Address:

Buyer: Tom Jones

Buyer: Mary Jones

Address:

Discussion

The beginning of the agreement sets forth the names of the parties to the agreement and names the sire and dam of the unborn foal.

1. This term sets forth where the mare will be located before and after the foal's birth. The location of the mare is important because the Buyer will want to ensure that the mare will have proper prenatal care and be at a facility that is equipped for and experienced with foaling.

2. The purchase price and the terms for payment must be clearly set forth. It is customary to pay the Seller a deposit upon entering into the agreement, with the remainder placed in some sort of an escrow-type account, such as the attorney client trust account set forth in the sample agreement.

3. Certain specific conditions should be set forth in this section, including references and restrictions to any specific markings or colorings peculiar to the breed in question that would make the foal undesirable for the Buyer's purpose.

4. This paragraph protects Buyer from any tax liens or other encumbrances that the Seller may have incurred.

5. Assures the Buyer that the Seller will not represent to anyone that the unborn foal is unsold.

6. Each party must give notice by the specific means set forth in this section whenever there is a change of address, a change in the mare's location, or any other material event that would affect the terms of the contract.

7. "Assignment" does not allow either party to assign his or her interest in this agreement to a third party unless the other party to the agreement consents in writing.

8. "Termination" sets forth the means by which both parties may agree not to go forward with the agreement for whatever reason. The conditions of termination must be mutually agreed upon so that neither party is in breach of the agreement.

9. Usually it will be the Seller who defaults, often because he or she has found someone who offers a higher price for the foal. It also could happen that the Buyer changes his or her mind for a variety of reasons. The default paragraph sets forth the consequences of one or the other party wanting out of the agreement.

10. It is important to establish and agree to the forum (state and locality) under which a legal action arising out of a dispute as to the agreement or the terms of the agreement can be taken. The forum state should be named in the body of the agreement. If possible, the forum should be convenient for both parties.

Instead of using the Governing Law clause, the parties may prefer to use Arbitration, because taking a party to court is very expensive and time consuming. Arbitration is not cheap, or easy, or speedy either, but it is still quicker and easier than litigation.

11. A liquidated damages clause primarily protects the Buyer in the event of a breach by the Seller. The Buyer is more at risk than the Seller when there is a breach, because the seller can still retain the foal and resell it should the buyer breach the agreement.

8

Installment Sale and Promissory Note

In an installment sale, the seller does not receive all the money at the time of the sale. For the installment sale described in this chapter, the seller signs a bill of sale stating he received a down payment plus a promissory note in payment for the purchase of the horse. A promissory note is an "I Owe You," in which the person who signs the note acknowledges that he owes money to someone else. The terms of the promissory note may vary. The amount owed may be payable on the demand of the person who holds the note or it may include a payment schedule.

The bill of sale and the promissory note are the two parts of this installment sale.

THE INSTALLMENT SALE

Example: Tony promises to buy his fiancée a horse named Tax Practice, but he does not have the ready cash for such a generous gift. Tony does have $2,500 for a down payment, and he could make regular payments. The seller, Jane, does not want to lose the sale but worries about releasing the horse without a guarantee that her money will be paid. For example, she does not want Tony to cease making payments or return the horse to her already-crowded barn if he breaks up with his fiancée.

The solution is to create a bill of sale transferring ownership of the horse to Tony in exchange for a down payment and a promissory note with a payment schedule. Keep in mind, however, that if the horse dies or is injured, Tony still owes on the note. In this case, the buyer (Tony) would be wise to insure a horse bought on credit. If the horse were to die or be humanely destroyed, the insurance would cover what he still owed and the seller would be assured the buyer has the money to finish paying for the horse even if the collateral dies. Many sellers require such insurance as a condition of an installment sale.

The installment sale requires a bill of sale specifically stating the receipt of the cash **plus** the promissory note as payment. The promissory note states the actual terms of the payment.

Security Interest and the Uniform Commercial Code

The sale of a horse is covered under the Uniform Commercial Code ("UCC"). Under the UCC, a security interest in the sale of a horse may be filed with the Secretary of State of a particular state to protect the seller's interest in the horse in case of buyer default or bankruptcy. Most states have adopted a version of the UCC.

Lien on Other Property as Additional Security

Although remedies are available through the courts in case of default or loss of value in the horse, to go through this process is costly and lengthy with no assurance of a positive result. Even filing a security interest, as noted above, does not insure the seller will get his or her money or the return of a healthy horse.

    Another alternative in an installment sale would be to take a lien on personal property such as the buyer's automobile. In the event the buyer either did not pay the balance due on the horse, did not maintain insurance, or neither horse or buyer could be located, the buyer would not be able to transfer ownership of his car until the seller's lien was satisfied (most states have strict automobile clear title regulations.) Another alternative would be a lien on the buyer's real property. Again, the buyer would never have clear title until the seller's lien was satisfied.

BILL OF SALE
WITH PROMISSORY NOTE

THIS BILL OF SALE, made this _____ , day of _____ , by and between _____ Jane O'Brien _____ , hereinafter called Seller, and _____ Tony _____ ___ Winner ___ hereinafter called Buyer.

   1. That in consideration of the payment of_____ Seven Thousand Five Hundred _____ Dollars ($7,500.00), Two Thousand Five Hundred Dollars ($2,500.00) in cash and a _____ Five Thousand Dollar ($5,000.00) _____ promissory note, by the Buyer to the Seller, the receipt of which is hereby acknowledged, said Seller does hereby bargain, sell, transfer, assign, and convey unto said Buyer, its successors and assigns, free and clear of all debts, liens, and encumbrances, the horse as described below:

     A. Name: Tax Practice

     B. Age: 4 years

     C. Color: Chestnut

     D. Breed: unreg. t.b.

     E. Sex: Gelding

     F. Size: 17 h.

   2. The Seller hereby represents that said horse hereby sold is its horse and that title is vested and that it has a good and perfect right to sell same, and that no debts, claims, obligations, or encumbrances exist on or against said horse.

   WITNESS, under the laws of the state of _____ , the hand of the Seller and Buyer.

WITNESS:

_____

_____
                          JANE O'BRIEN

                          Address

                          Telephone

                          TONY WINNER

                          Address

                          Telephone

Discussion of Installment Bill of Sale

Like a regular bill of sale, this sale states the name of the two parties. If either is a corporation, the words "a corporation" and the state of incorporation should follow.

Next, the consideration is stated, that is, the total price followed by how much was paid in cash and how much was paid by a promissory note. The seller claims she is transferring the horse free and clear with no debts attached for the horse, which is described. The pronoun "it" is used to avoid confusion with "he" or "she."

Then the seller states that she completely owns the horse and has the right to sell it. Both parties sign, with addresses and phone numbers. There is a space for witnesses to assure the verity of the signatures. Witnesses are not always required, but may prevent any denials in the future. In any event, they are always a good safeguard in any contract.

THE PROMISSORY NOTE

The agreement is made between Tony and Jane. Tony buys the horse form Jane for $2,500 in cash and a $5,000 balance. This note covers the balance. Without this note, the seller's alternative would be to retain an interest in the horse. When a person borrows money from a bank to buy a car, the bank records a lien on the car until the loan is fully repaid. In essence, the same procedure is followed when a horse is sold on the installment basis. Yet, the situation is more complex, because horses are easily injured. A person might sell a horse for $50,000 but, within the year, the horse's resale value could drop to $20,000, or less because of injury.

With a promissory note, the seller is in a much more secure position than with a lien on the horse.

SAMPLE

PROMISSORY NOTE

THIS AGREEMENT is made between _____ Tony Winner _____ (the "Undersigned") and _____ Jane O'Brien _____ .

1. Consideration

FOR VALUE RECEIVED, __TONY__ __WINNER_____ does hereby promise to pay to the order of __JANE__ __O'BRIEN_____ the sum of _Five_ _Thousand___ ($ _5,000.00_) Dollars, together with interest on the unpaid principal balance at the rate of _____Ten_____ Percent (_10_ %) per annum from the date hereof in installments beginning on _____ _____and on the first of each month thereafter in the amount of $__106.24____ until the entire principal balance is paid in full or until _sixty (60) months_ thereafter, at which time the amount then owing shall be due.

2. Payment Terms

The monthly payments are calculated on an amortization schedule of _____five_____ years and the full amount then owing shall be due_____five_____ years from the date of the first payment, unless otherwise accelerated under the terms and conditions hereof. Both principal and interest shall be payable at the address of _____JANE O'BRIEN_____ at _Fireplace Road, East Hampton,_ _New York 11937_____ , or at such other address as may be designated from time to time by written notification to the Undersigned by the holder hereof.

3. Prepayment

The Undersigned shall have the right to prepay, at any time or times, without penalty, all or any part of the balance of the principal hereof. Any such prepayment shall be applied first to any unpaid interest accrued hereunder and then to the principal, in which case the amounts due with respect to succeeding interest payments hereunder shall be adjusted accordingly.

4. Default

In the event (any of which events shall be deemed an "event of default"): (a) the Undersigned shall fail to make any payment of principal or interest when due hereunder and such failure shall have continued for ten (10) days after written notice of such default by the holder hereof, or (b) any voluntary petition by, or involuntary petition against, the Undersigned shall be filed under any chapter of the Federal Bankruptcy Act, or any proceeding involving the Undersigned shall be instituted under any other law relating to the relief of debtors, and such petition or proceeding shall not be vacated within ten (10) days thereafter, or (c) the Undersigned shall make any assignment for the benefit of creditors, or (d) a judgment shall be entered against the Undersigned in any court of record and shall not be satisfied within five (5) days thereafter, then the holder hereof, in his, his/her, or their sole discretion may declare this Promissory Note to be due forthwith, and the same shall thereupon become immediately due and payable in full, all without any presentment, demand, or notice of any kind, which are hereby waived.

5. Rights of Holder

No delay or omission on the part of the holder hereof in the exercise of any right or remedy shall operate as a waiver thereof, and no single or partial exercise by the holder of any right or remedy shall preclude other or further exercise of any right or remedy.

6. Remedies

The Undersigned hereby authorizes any attorney of any court within the State of _____ or elsewhere to confess judgment against the Undersigned at any time after this Promissory Note is due (whether upon normal maturity or acceleration hereunder), hereby waiving all exemptions, for the principal amount of this Promissory Note and interest and attorney's fees and court costs. If this Promissory Note is referred to an attorney for collection, then there shall be added to the amount due and owing hereunder reasonable attorney's fees of not less than 15% or such amount as any Court in which an action is filed deems to be reasonable, plus costs of collection.

7. Waiving of Defenses

The Undersigned hereby waives presentment, demand, notice of dishonor, protest, and all other demands and notices whatsoever in connection with the delivery, acceptance, performance, and enforcement of this Note.

8. (a) Governing Law.

This Agreement shall be construed in accordance with and shall be governed by the laws of the State of _____ .
Any legal action must be brought in the county/municipality of_____.

OR

(b) Arbitration.

The parties to this Agreement mutually agree that any and all disputes arising in connection with this Agreement shall be settled and determined by binding arbitration conducted in accordance with the then existing rules of the American Arbitration Association by one or more arbitrators appointed in accordance with said rules. Said arbitration shall take place in
_____(municipality)
_____ (state).

9. Entire Agreement.

This constitutes the entire Agreement between the parties. Any modifications or additions MUST be in writing and signed by all parties to this Agreement. No oral modifications or additions will be considered to be part of this Agreement unless reduced to writing and signed by all parties.

Executed this _____ day of
_____(month),
_____ (year).

_____
TONY WINNER

_____
Address

_____

_____
Telephone

Discussion of Promissory Note

First, the parties are named.

1. This section states the amount this note is worth. It is like a check "pay to the order of," and it is equally negotiable. It could be endorsed over to someone else to collect on it. If the seller needed cash now, he could sell the note at a discounted price.

2. The payments begin on a specified date for a specified number of months with the amount of the monthly payment stated. The address of the payee is also included subject to change. The payee may move or transfer the note to another person.

3. This section allows prepayment at any time with the order of application, first to interest and then principal.

4. If Tony doesn't pay as scheduled and receives written notice from Jane, he has ten days to pay the installment, or Jane can declare the note immediately due. Furthermore, the note is immediately due if Tony declares bankruptcy, applies for any other legal protection, or does not seem able to pay on this note as specified and does not prove otherwise within the number of days stated.

5. No matter what Jane, the holder of this note, does, Tony still owes the money. If she dies, he owes the money to her legatee.

6. In this section, Tony agrees that Jane's attorney has the right to collect the payment if overdue, and Tony will be liable for any additional costs necessary to collect on this note.

7. Tony relinquishes any right to use defenses to avoid paying this note. For example, he can't claim the horse isn't worth the money.

8. The Governing Law is named and the venue if the parties take legal action, or an arbitration clause is used.

Finally, the note is dated and signed and completed with the address and telephone number of the person who owes the money.

9

Purchase Agreement

A purchase agreement is a contract in which the buyer has made a down payment on the purchase of a horse. The seller and buyer both agree to the terms of the sale and agree on the date of the closing when the purchase price will be paid in full and the ownership of the horse will be transferred to the buyer.

Example: George Horseman buys an expensive show pony. He will pay in full before delivery but makes a down payment to the owner to hold the horse for him. He wants to be certain that the purchase price will not be changed between the time the deposit is made and the pay off. He also needs assurance that the pony will not be sold to anyone else, and that the seller is responsible for the pony until the payment is made in full, in two weeks time. Additionally, if the pony were to die in the meantime, George wants his down payment refunded. George prepares a purchase agreement.

SAMPLE

PURCHASE AGREEMENT

THIS AGREEMENT is made between _____ George Horseman _____ , residing at
Westriver, New York _____ ("Buyer") and
Jane Rider _____ , residing at _Southriver, New York_
_____("Seller") for the purchase described below:

Name:	Flower Pot
Age:	10 years
Color:	Bay
Breed:	Anglo Arab
Sex:	Mare
Size:	14 h 2"

1. Purchase Price
For the total sum of $____ 50,000.00 ____ , Seller agrees to sell and Buyer agrees to buy said horse based on the terms to follow.

2. Payment Terms
The Buyer agrees to pay $_____ 10,000.00 _____ , as a deposit on the execution of this Agreement _____ and the balance due of $ _____ 40,000.00 ____ on the day of delivery, no more than 14 days from the date of this Agreement.

3. Warranties
   (a) Seller covenants that he/she is the lawful owner of said horse; that he/she has the right to sell said horse; and that he/she will warrant and defend the horse against lawful claims and demands of all persons.
   (b) Seller makes no other promises, express or implied, including the warranties of fitness for a particular purpose unless further provided in this Agreement.
   (c) Seller warrants the following: this horse is qualified for the Devon Horse Show and has a permanent size pony card.
   (d) Buyer waives any claim for damage should said horse fail to meet the above warranties at the time of delivery, unless such defect is discovered within _____ ten (10) _____ days from delivery to Buyer.

4. Transfer of Ownership
Once Seller has received payment in full, Seller shall transfer all owner and registration papers of the horse at his own expense to the Buyer.

5. Risk of Loss
Seller assumes all risk of loss until the Buyer takes delivery or until the Buyer begins transfer of the horse, whichever comes first.

6. (a) Governing Law.

The terms of this Agreement shall be governed by the laws of the State of _____ .
Any legal action must be brought in _____ county/municipality.

OR

(b) Arbitration.

The parties to this Agreement mutually agree that any and all disputes arising in connection with this Agreement shall be settled and determined by binding arbitration conducted in accordance with the then existing rules of the American Arbitration Association by one or more arbitrators appointed in accordance with said rules. Said arbitration shall take place in _____(municipality), _____(state).

7. Breach

Either party may nullify this Agreement if the other party breaches a material term of this Agreement.
The wronged party may recover reasonable attorney's fees and court costs.

8. Entire Agreement.

This constitutes the entire Agreement between the parties. Any modifications or additions MUST be in writing and signed by all parties to this Agreement. No oral modifications or additions will be considered to be part of this Agreement unless reduced to writing and signed by all parties.

Executed this _____ day of _____ (month),_____ (year).

SELLER: BUYER:

_____   _____
Signature   Signature

_____   _____
Address   Address

Discussion

Again, it is very important to get the full names, addresses, and description of the horse. The age and size of the horse are material because show horses or ponies are often bought for their size in certain hunter divisions. Age is another significant factor because a horse described as a ten-year-old may have a different value as a sixteen-year-old.

1.   The purchase price must be clearly stated here. There have been cases in which sudden interest is sparked in a horse because of winnings or breeding, and a seller may be tempted to raise the price after the contract has been signed.

2.   To protect the seller, the payment terms ensure that a cash transaction does not drag out and become an unintended installment sale.

3.   This section of warranties is one of the most sensitive areas.
   (a) The seller states that he owns the horse and has the right to sell it. This is a crucial protection to the buyer.
   (b) On the other hand, the seller protects himself by saying "what you see is what you get" with the emphasis on nothing more. In other words, "buyer beware" is the basic premise.
   (c) If the seller does include any assurances as to soundness or suitability, these are explicitly listed. The buyer may require a written statement of the facts he is relying on as the basis of this purchase, in this case the qualification for the Devon Horse Show and the size of the pony.
   (d) The ten-day period is not a trial of the horse. The contract will be void only if the buyer or seller has not fulfilled his part of the bargain.

4.   The owner is responsible for transferring papers and any necessary notices to the buyer.

5.   The risk of losing the horse is assumed by the buyer as soon as he takes delivery. The actual point of delivery can vary. If the buyer boards where he bought the horse, this date would begin when payment is made in full. If the seller delivers the horse, the risk passes when the horse arrives on the buyer's farm or when the buyer himself picks up the horse with his van or his agent's van.

6.   The state of Governing Law and the county where any legal action would take place are named or an arbitration clause is used.

7.   George can declare this agreement null and void if the seller breaks a material term of the agreement. The court and attorney's costs are paid for by the seller if the buyer is forced into court to get his money refunded.

The contract has no validity until both parties have signed.

10

Lease

A lease is a contract in which a person pays for the use of a horse over a set period. The person who leases the horse assumes the responsibilities of the horse as if he or she owned it under the terms of the agreement.

Leasing high-quality horses has become a popular alternative to the high cost of purchasing.

Example: Norma wants to lease a show horse for her grandson, Fred, and wants to spread the lease payments out over the year. Because the owner wants to be sure the horse has the same care as he has been receiving, the owner includes some special instructions in the Agreement and is also requiring Norma to purchase mortality and loss of use insurance on the horse. Norma would like the option of renewing the lease or buying the horse, should the owner want to lease him again or sell him. The following lease meets all these concerns.

SAMPLE LEASE AGREEMENT

60

SAMPLE

LEASE AGREEMENT

This Lease is made _____ (date) between __John Rider__
residing at __Sunshine Road, Gomer, OK__ (hereinafter referred to as "Lessor"), and __Norma Edwards__, residing at __Fireplace Road, Gomer, OK__ (hereinafter referred to as "Lessee").

1. Term.
(a) The term of this Lease shall be for a period of one year, beginning_____ (date) and ending no later than _____ (date), or as otherwise provided for herein.
(b) Lessee shall have the option to return the horse to Lessor prior to the end of the lease term, should circumstances dictate and providing lease fees are fully paid up to the time the horse is returned. In no case will any fees be refunded for unused lease time.

2. Description.
This Lease covers the horse(s) described in this section below.

   A. Name: Tax & Spend
   B. Age: 10 years
   C. Breed: Peruvian Paso
   D. Sex: Gelding
   E. Size: 15 hands

3. Consideration/Payment.
Lessee shall pay a fee of _____Five Thousand Dollars ($5,000.00)_____,
payable as follows:

Payment	Date
$1,250.00	January 1, (year)
$1,250.00	April 1, (year)
$1,250.00	July 1, (year)
$1,250.00	October 1, (year)

4. Uses of Horse and Limitations.
Lessee covenants not to use the horse for any purpose other than set forth: __shall be ridden in lesson and schooling sessions as necessary and shown at horse shows__.
Lessor promises that said horse is capable and suited for said purpose. Lessor explicitly denies the right to any other part for any sublease agreement, barring all other riders except the Lessee's instructor or chosen professional rider where appropriate.
Lessee shall not have the right to relocate the horse, except as is usual for competition purposes, without the written consent of the Lessor.

5. Instructions for Care.

Lessee will follow all practices consistent with quality care___on the horse show circuit_____ at Lessee's own expense. Lessee shall provide all necessary veterinarian and blacksmith needs at Lessee's own expense. In addition said horse requires:

(a) a double stall when vanning_____
(b) shavings for bedding_____
(c) pads on front shoes_____
(d) daily turn-out alone when not showing___

[Grain rations and hay plus stall size can be stated here.]

6. Risk of Loss and Insurance.

(a) Lessee assumes risk of loss or injury to said horse(s), barring an act of the Lessor or Lessor's agent, contractors, or employees.

(b) Lessee shall at his/her own expense at all times during the term of this lease maintain in force a policy or policies of mortality and loss of use insurance written by one or more responsible insurance carriers acceptable to Lessor. A copy of said policy must be mailed to Lessor within a month of taking delivery of the horse.

The liability under such policy shall be not less than___Thirty Thousand Dollars_____ ($30,000.00)_____ payable to the Lessor as sole beneficiary.

7. Ownership.

Lessor warrants that he/she owns said horse free and clear and has the right to execute this Lease.

8. Options.

(a) Lessee has the option to renew this Lease for an additional___twelve___(12) months if a request is made in writing___thirty (30)___days prior to the expiration of this Lease, provided the horse is available for a lease.

(b) If horse is placed up for sale, the Lessee has the right of first refusal to purchase said horse within_____two_____(2) months of the expiration of said lease for a price not to exceed Fifty Thousand Dollars ($50,000.00)_____ .

9. Covenant Not to Encumber.

Lessee agrees not to encumber said horse(s) with any lien, charge, or related claim and to hold Lessor harmless therefrom.

10. Default.

Upon material breach of this Agreement, Lessor reserves the right to remove such horse without incurring any responsibility to Lessee.

This Agreement is terminated upon a breach of any material term and the other party has the right to collect all reasonable fees and costs from the breaching party.

11. (a) Governing Law.

This Agreement shall be construed in accordance with and shall be governed by the laws of the State of _____. Any legal action must be brought in the county/municipality of _____ .

OR

(b) Arbitration.

The parties to this Agreement mutually agree that any and all disputes arising in connection with this Agreement shall be settled and determined by binding arbitration conducted in accordance with the then existing rules of the American Arbitration Association by one or more arbitrators appointed in accordance with said rules. Said arbitration shall take place in _____ (municipality), _____ (state).

12. Entire Agreement.

This constitutes the entire Agreement between the parties. Any modifications or additions MUST be in writing and signed by all parties to this Agreement. No oral modifications or additions will be considered to be part of this Agreement unless reduced to writing and signed by all parties.

Signed this _____ day of _____ (month), _____ (year).

LESSOR: LESSEE:

_____   _____
Signature   Signature

_____   _____
Address   Address

_____   _____
Telephone   Telephone

Discussion

The beginning of the lease names the parties, sets the date the lease was drafted, and includes addresses of both parties.

1. (a) The term of the lease sets the time span of the arrangement. A lease might cover a single horse show or run as long as several years. Because horses are prone to injuries or junior riders may need to upgrade their horses after a year, a show season or one year is the most common term.

2. The description of the horse is a basic part of the agreement. If several horses are leased, for instance, for a summer camp or for a school program, descriptions of all the horses would be included here.

3. This section clarifies the fee and the schedule of the payments. The lessor can threaten to take the horse back if the payment is not made.

Owners are often looking for good homes for horses they don't want to sell, so horses or ponies suitable for local shows are sometimes available for "free leases." The lessee pays all expenses, but there is no "lease fee." This way, the owner knows the horse or pony is well maintained, but they don't have the monthly expense. If this is the case, a $1.00 consideration as the lease fee should be stated here.

4. This section clarifies the scope of the horse's use under the lease. The owner/lessor warrants in turn that the horse is sound and suited for the purpose as represented. He may deny here the use of the horse by other riders. This lessor likes John's instructor and wants the horse to stay in the same barn where the care is excellent. She does not want the horse subleased to another stable.

This clause also allows for the lessee to return the horse to the lessor during the terms of the lease, but the lease fees must be fully paid up to the time the horse is returned and any fees paid beyond the date when the horse is returned will not be refunded to the lessee.

5. The "Instructions for Care" vary in specificity depending on past practices, the geographic area, and the purpose and quality of the lessee. Veterinary and blacksmith fees are included here at the lessee's expense. Sometimes a lessor will require preapproval of the boarding facility.

Special instructions are listed, stating idiosyncracies or directions necessary to the horse's well-being; for example, he panics without a double stall when vanning, eats straw bedding, and needs pads.

6. The "Risk of Loss and Insurance" section is a protection for both parties. The lessee assumes the cost of the premium.

7. The lessor must own the horse. This seems like a redundant paragraph but it protects the lessee, and there have been cases in which agents, unauthorized by the owners, have leased horses.

8. (a) The lessee may request an option to renew the lease, provided the lessor/owner does not choose to sell the horse or use the horse for other purposes.

The lessee may want to tie down the owner in the first year of the lease to the maximum renewal rate. Here they do not set a renewal price. Norma is willing to pay fair market value.

(b) In addition, the right of first refusal is an important clause to the lessee since she has chosen a horse she might like to own.

In this event, the lessee has the right to match an offer from a willing buyer on the open market, and here Norma has protected herself by capping the price at $50,000. The lessor may not agree to this cap if the horse is relatively unproven at the beginning of the lease because, potentially, the horse may be worth more.

9. The lessee must promise to pay the bills. For instance, a problem could arise if the person leasing the horse runs behind on the board bill. In that case, the stable may place a lien on the horse and the true owner cannot retrieve the horse without paying the delinquent barn bill.

10. If either party breaks the agreement on a basic term, then the wronged party collects damages. If the lessee is at fault, the lessor can retrieve the horse. A written notice and warning is strongly advised before either party reverts to self-help. Courts may interpret a material breach quite differently than an owner whose feelings have been hurt.

11. The state of Governing Law and the county where any legal action would take place are named or an arbitration clause is used.

Finally, the agreement is dated and signed with names, addresses, and telephone numbers.

11

Lease — Breeding Services of a Stallion

The lease of a stallion is basically no different in concept from the lease of a school horse or a show horse. One person or persons lease a horse for a set fee for a specific term. The only difference lies in the agreement itself, because the owner and the lessee must include provisions in the contract relevant to stallions and breeding practices.

Example: For tax purposes and because they love horses, the Riders decide to run a small breeding operation. They believe there is a shortage of large athletic Thoroughbreds raised in this country for showing and hunting. In response to this perceived need, they have bought large registered mares. They need a quality stallion but the horse they want is out of their price range. However, the owner is willing to lease the stallion to them for a year. They want the horse for one year to see if the arrangement is successful. They need to make monthly payments because they do not want to deplete their working capital in the first month of the year. They are willing to reserve some breeding rights for the owner of the stallion. They recognize that stallions can be dangerous and plan to buy liability insurance in the event there is an accident caused by the stallion on their property. The Riders are familiar with this stallion. They are anxious to get a signed contract with the owner. The following lease should work for them.

SAMPLE

LEASE — BREEDING SERVICES OF A STALLION

Lease made <u>January 1 (year)</u> between <u>Stableview, Inc.</u>, a corporation organized and existing under the laws of the State of <u>New York</u>, with principal place of business at <u>99 Horse Avenue</u>, City of <u>Riverhead</u>, County of <u>Suffolk</u>, State of <u>New York</u>, herein referred to as Lessor, and <u>Jane Rider</u> of <u>999 Saddle Road</u>, City of <u>Fieldstown</u>, County of <u>Suffolk</u>, State of <u>Maryland</u>, herein referred to as Lessee.

Lessor hereby leases to Lessee, who is engaged in the business of breeding horses for the show ring and hunt field, the below described stallion. In consideration of the terms herein set forth, the parties agree as follows:

1. Description and Delivery of Stallion.
<u>Lessor</u> agrees to deliver Lessor's Thoroughbred stallion ("Stallion") herein described to stand for breeding services at <u>Jane Rider's Mountainview Farm</u> at the above described location.

Name	Age	Color	Size	Jockey Club Reg. No.
Cosmic Hill	10 years	Bay	17 h	J99999

2. Term.
The Term of this lease shall be for a period beginning <u>January 1, (year)</u>, and ending no later than <u>December 31, (year)</u>, or as otherwise provided for herein.

3. Payment.
Lessee shall pay a fee of <u>Ten Thousand</u> dollars ($ <u>10,000.00</u>) for the stud services of Stallion, payable in <u>Four</u> (<u>4</u>) installments of <u>Two Thousand Five Hundred</u> dollars ($ <u>2,500.00</u>). The payment schedule is as follows:

Date	Amount
1/1/	$2,500.00
4/15/	$2,500.00
8/15/	$2,500.00
1/1/	$2,500.00

Payments not made within ten (10) days of due date will accrue interest on the unpaid balance at 12% per annum.

4. Care and Service by Stallion.

(a) Lessee agrees to provide adequate feed, water, shelter, care, maintenance, and veterinary care as required in a manner consistent with good Thoroughbred practices in the County of __Suffolk__ _____ , State of ___New York___ at Lessee's expense. This care includes annual vaccinations and regular shoeing and worming. Any specific provisions as to feed, stall size, and turnout follow:

(1)

(2)

(b) Lessee covenants that Stallion shall not service in excess of ___Thirty___ (__30__) mares during the breeding season herein described. Lessee will provide a written report of all breedings every sixty (60) days.

(c) Lessor reserves ___five___ breeding rights with no fee charged, other than boarding charges on the mares.

5. Uses of Stallion.

Lessee covenants not to use the Stallion for any purpose other than breeding as herein provided.

6. Assignment.

Lessee shall not assign this lease, or any interest herein, nor sublet Stallion or in any manner permit the use of the Stallion for any purpose other than as herein set forth.

7. Insurance.

(a) Lessee shall at his own expense, at all times during term of this lease, maintain in force a policy, written by one or more insurance carriers acceptable to Lessor which shall insure Lessor against liability for injury to or death of persons or damage or loss of property occurring in or about the premises on which the Stallion is used for breeding. The amount of coverage per person, per accident, and for property damage must be approved by Lessor. In addition he must receive a copy of said policy within ten days of its effective date.

(b) Lessee agrees to insure Stallion for the lease period with mortality or loss of use insurance purchased from a company, approved by Lessor, for the sum of $___60,000.00___ , said insurance payable to Lessor as beneficiary.

8. Miscellaneous Expenses.

Lessee will be responsible to pay all expenses incidental to or consequential of leasing Stallion as if he/she owned Stallion for said term.

9. Permission to Inspect.

Lessor may inspect Stallion at any and all times, and Lessee agrees to follow strictly all reasonable instructions, regarding feed, care, handling, and breeding of Stallion.

10. Termination of Agreement.

(a) At termination for whatever reason, Lessee shall redeliver Stallion to Lessor at above described address at Lessee's expense.

(b) Agreement is terminated on fifteen (15) days written notice if there is a material breach of terms set forth herein.

(c) Any reasonable attorney's fees or court costs incurred as a result of such breach shall be paid by breaching party.

(d) Agreement shall be terminated upon presentation of evidence by a veterinarian that Stallion is unable to successfully impregnate mares for whatever reason. Lessee shall have no right to refund and all payments are still due and payable in a timely fashion.

11. Lessor's Lien.

Lessee grants Lessor a first lien on any foals produced under the terms hereof, under
New York _____ law for all unpaid charges on account.

12. (a) Governing Law.

All terms and covenants of this Agreement shall be enforced and constructed in accordance with
the laws of the State of _____New York_____. Any legal action must be brought in
_____(county/municipality).

OR

(b) Arbitration.

The parties to this Agreement mutually agree that any and all disputes arising in connection with
this Agreement shall be settled and determined by binding arbitration conducted in accordance with the
then existing rules of the American Arbitration Association by one or more arbitrators appointed in
accordance with said rules. Said arbitration shall take place in _____
(municipality),_____ (state).

13. Entire Agreement.

This constitutes the entire Agreement between the parties. Any modifications or additions MUST
be in writing and signed by all parties to this Agreement. No oral modifications or additions will be
considered to be part of this Agreement unless reduced to writing and signed by all parties.

IN WITNESS WHEREOF, the parties hereto have executed this Lease Agreement as of the day
and year above written.

LESSOR: LESSEE:

_____   _____
Signature   Signature

_____
Name of Stallion

_____
Registration Number

Discussion

The Lease begins with an identification of the parties. If the lessor is not a corporation, the person's name or the partnership would be given here. The addresses appear also. Next, the lessee's purpose in leasing the stallion is stated. Here the lessee is planning a breeding operation for show horses and hunters. Often the purpose is to produce race horses.

1. The first terms state who is responsible for delivery of the stallion with a full description of the horse.

2. The term of the lease is set. Here it is for one year.

3. This section states the payment schedule with four installments on a quarterly basis. There is an interest charge for late payments. This gives the Riders a more comfortable financial commitment instead of requiring them to pay a lump sum at the beginning.

4. (a) The "Care and Service" terms are set out here. The standard of care language includes the need for annual vaccinations and regular shoeing. The lessor can also add directions for feeding, stall size, and turnout.

   (b) The lease specifies the number of servicings a season with a report due after a two-month period. Here the parties may decide whether the stallion can be used to breed outside mares. If so, the owner may receive a percentage of the stud fee.

   (c) The owner also reserves a number of breeding rights for his own horses.

5. The stallion may not be used for any purpose not intended by the lessor. If he agrees that the stallion may be shown, raced, or even ridden, this provision must be stated specifically.

6. The lessee cannot sell or give his contract to someone else without the agreement of the lessor. Usually, a right to assignment is limited by the owner's approval, if allowed at all.

7. (a) The importance of insurance cannot be underestimated. The owner must protect himself from liability in the event the stallion injures a person or destroys property. He needs assurance from the lessee of adequate coverage and may specify a dollar amount per person and per accident. Insurance companies can advise you here.

   (b) The stallion is also insured for a set amount with the lessor as beneficiary. The lessee may require a prorated return on the lease fee if the stallion dies or is seriously injured so as to decrease his value as a stud within a certain date. (See discussion on insurance under the Lease form.) The parties may split costs here or determine who pays the premiums.

8. Under "Miscellaneous Expenses," the lessee assumes all incidental costs not otherwise listed, such as a new halter, blanket, or fly spray.

9. The "Permission to Inspect" is a protection for both parties. The stallion's care must be monitored, and the lessee is responsible for following the lessor's guidelines. The owner should be familiar with the lessee, his stable practices, and his reputation before entrusting the stallion to him. He should be certain the fencing and stabling arrangements are adequate and that a competent professional is handling the breeding operation. He should also not hesitate to exercise his option to inspect the horse during the term of the lease.

10. (a) If the agreement is terminated, the party named (here the lessee) must return the horse to the lessor at the lessee's expense.

(b) The agreement is ended if one party breaks a material term of the agreement and is notified of this breach in writing.

(c) The attorney's fees and court costs are paid by the breaching party.

(d) The agreement is also ended if the stallion is impotent for whatever reason. Here the lessee was familiar with the horse, and could have the horse's fertility analyzed by a veterinarian. The lessee may require a statement of the stallion's past record. Sometimes, the refund policy is modified for infertility, but the lessors are often unwilling to assume this risk.

11. The "Lessor's Lien" is a provision giving the lessor a security interest in foals if the lessee doesn't make the payments. This would not be possible, however, if the stallion were breeding mares not owned by the lessee. Otherwise, the lessor could terminate the lease and/or sue for payment.

12. The "Governing Law" is applicable in the event of a conflict of state laws, usually if the parties have different state residences or places of business. This is a standard clause in all contracts.

Instead of using the Governing Law clause, the parties may prefer to use an Arbitration clause, because taking a party to court is very expensive and time-consuming. Arbitration is not cheap, or easy, or speedy either, but it is still quicker and easier than litigation.

Finally, the contract is executed by signatures. This agreement is a fairly simple version. Several other options may be included:

- The lessor must sign by a certain date all breeding certificates, duly executed for whatever registry is applicable. This clause is to ensure that all offspring are properly registered.

- The live foal guarantees and breedback rights may be specified. In the event of a barren mare or a foal not standing, rebreeding rights are usually provided with the dates specified for the current season or the following year.

- The lessor may reserve an option to lease the horse again for the following year at a set price. Usually, a written notice of this intent is required, and the lessee must inform the lessor of his intent within a certain number of days before the lease in effect expires.

12

Breeding Contracts

A breeding contract is an agreement between the owner of a mare, who wishes to breed the mare, and the owner of a stud farm, who will take the mare for a specified time, breed the mare and care for the mare through the birth of the foal. A breeding contract should be executed by the parties before the mare is delivered to the stud farm.

Although all breeding contracts can be quite simple in nature, it is recommended that they be drafted to address as many contingencies and details as possible. It may be surprising to know that many disputes arise out of a breeding agreement. To avoid this possibility, a written agreement with all the terms and conditions specified within will provide protection to both parties.

A breeding contract should be executed by the parties before the mare is delivered to the stud farm. A detailed mare information form should accompany the breeding or booking agreement.

Most reputable stud farms require various health certificates before accepting the mare to be bred. For this reason, most breeding contracts are executed prior to the delivery of the mare to the breeding facility and are contingent upon the mare's clean bill of health.

Since the breeding contract often involves the boarding of the mare and later also the foal, liability issues arise in the event that the mare or foal are injured or die while being boarded and cared for at the stud farm.

One critical issue which must be addressed and agreed to by the parties in the breeding agreement is the definition of what comprises a "live foal." Common definitions can range from very narrow to very broad. Therefore, the parties must agree to one definition and include it in their written agreement.

The breeding contract should contain some sort of waiver of liability. This can be accomplished by inserting clauses in the breeding contract that address (1) which party will assume the risk of loss or injury to the mare, (2) whether insurance will be required to be obtained in the event of loss or injury, and (3) whether owner of mare shall indemnify and hold harmless the owner of the stallion.

SAMPLE

BREEDING CONTRACT FOR STALLION

THIS AGREEMENT is made by and between ___John Horseman, dba Stableview___
Farms_____ , residing at _____ ,
hereinafter referred to as "Owner of Stallion," and___Jane Rider, dba Far Hills Ranch ,
located at _____ , hereinafter referred to as "Owner of Mare."

1. Fees.
   a. In consideration of_____One Thousand and Five Hundred ($1,500)____ dollars
(plus applicable sales tax), Owner of Stallion hereby agrees to breed his stallion___March to____
Time_____ to ____Windsong_____ , a mare owned by ___Jane____
Rider, dba Far Hills Ranch_____ .
   b. Owner of Mare agrees to pay said $ _1,500_ on the dates indicated below:

Date   Amount

_____   _____

_____   _____

_____   _____

   c. In the event that Owner of Mare's mare does not take and become in foal, Owner of Stallion
agrees to breed said mare again for $_____additional consideration at any time prior to
_____ .
   d. In the event said mare does not deliver a live foal, Owner of Stallion agrees to give Owner of
Mare the right to an additional service to said mare (at any time within_____ months) from the last
date of breeding said mare under this contract.
   Owner of Stallion shall have no further liability hereunder for servicing said mare. For the purposes of this Agreement, "Live Foal" means "standing and nursing" for a period of at least
twenty-four hours after post-birth .

2. Health/Other Requirements.
   Owner of Mare warrants that said mare is free from disease or infection that could be transmitted
to said stallion, and agrees to provide and pay for a veterinarian certificate, showing such freedom of
disease or infection.

3. Boarding/Veterinary Care.
   In addition to the above charge for breeding, Owner of Mare agrees to pay the following:
a. $15 a day for feed and board;
b. $10 a day for exercise of said mare as described below:
c. Owner of Stallion agrees to provide the following for the fees indicated;
      i. Feed:
            Two flakes of hay per feeding;
            _1/2 lb.____ of grain per feeding;
            _Two_____ feedings per day.

d. Stall:
Box Stall with outside paddock.

e. Turn-out/Pasture:
Daily turnout in pasture during first and second trimesters of pregnancy.

f. Owner of Stallion agrees to use reasonable care and caution for said mare while in his possession or control, pursuant to this Agreement, and is authorized to obtain any necessary veterinarian or farrier care as required, but only after taking steps to contact Owner of Mare without success. Owner is to provide local veterinarian of her choice and nearest veterinary hospital of her prior authorization to admit and treat said mare and to provide veterinarian and hospital with assurance of full payment for any and all treatment so made.

4. Liability.
Owner of Mare agrees to assume the risk of injury, sickness, or death to said mare except where caused by negligence of Owner of Stallion, his agents, officers, contractors, or employees.

5. Indemnification.
Owner of Mare agrees to indemnify and hold Owner of Stallion harmless for any loss or injury due to acts of said mare while on premises or under control of Owner of Stallion except where caused by negligence of Owner of Stallion, his agents, officers, contractors, or employees.

6. Insurance.
To protect against said loss or injury, Owner of Mare agrees to secure liability insurance in the amount of $1,000,000 for personal injury per accident, and $500,000 per injury, and $300,000 property damage and to provide a certificate of insurance having named Owner of Stallion additional insured.

7. Rebreeding.
If prior to the breeding of said mare or after the mare has been bred but not come in foal, said stallion or mare dies or becomes unfit for service as so declared by a licensed veterinarian, then this Agreement shall become null and void and all monies paid by Owner of Mare, not including expenses, shall be refunded.

Or, mare owner shall have no right to a refund hereunder, but shall have the option of using the following stallions of the owner at the charges indicated:

Hit the Mark

Sky's the Limit

8. Breeding Certificate.
Owner of Stallion agrees to execute all necessary documents of the registration of the offspring of the breeding and should he fail or be unable to do so, [Name of Agent if Registry permits] is hereby authorized to so execute on behalf of Owner of Stallion as his agent, only if the involved Registry will accept this agency appointment.

9. Termination.
Either party may terminate this Agreement for failure of the other party to meet any material terms of this Agreement. In the case of any default or breach by one party, the other party shall have the right to recover attorney's fees and court costs incurred as a result of said default.

10. (a) Governing Law.

This Agreement is governed and shall be construed under the laws of the State of _____ . Any legal action must be brought in _____ (county/municipality).

OR

(b) Arbitration.

The parties to this Agreement mutually agree that any and all disputes arising in connection with this Agreement will be settled and determined by binding arbitration conducted in accordance with the then existing rules of the American Arbitration Association by one or more arbitrators appointed in accordance with said rules. Said arbitration shall take place in _____ (municipality), _____ (state).

11. Entire Agreement.

This constitutes the entire Agreement between the parties. Any modifications or additions MUST be in writing and signed by all parties to this Agreement. No oral modifications or additions will be considered to be part of this Agreement unless reduced to writing and signed by all parties.

Dated: _____ , _____ (year).

_____
John Horseman, dba Stableview Farms

_____
(Address)

_____
Jane Rider, dba Far Hills Ranch

_____
(Address)

Discussion

The names of the owner of the stallion and the owner of the mare appear at the beginning of the document.

1. The amount of stud fees to be paid and the times at which they are to be paid are set forth in detail here. The terms in this clause are negotiable and are left blank because every situation is different. The terms with regard to schedule of payments and number of breedings will depend upon the status and popularity of the stallion and custom can vary from one breed to another. For example, if a stallion is very well known and has a fully booked season, the owner of the stallion will probably not allow rebreeding or only a very limited number of rebreedings. The owner of such a stallion may require the complete breeding fee to be paid up front and may charge extra for rebreedings, as provided for in clause 1c. The parties' mutual understanding as to what constitutes a "live foal" should be set forth in detail here (clause 1d).

2. The owner of the stallion wants to make certain that the mare is healthy and in good condition to be bred.

3. The kind of care that the mare's owner wishes her to have while at the stud farm and the kind of care the stud farm agrees to give is explained in great detail here.

4. The stud farm and the mare owner agree as to who will assume liability in the event of the mare's being injured, becoming ill, or dying.

5. The owner of the mare agrees to indemnify and hold harmless the stallion owner in the event that the mare causes injury to another horse or to a person or property, except where the stallion owner or the various named persons under his control are negligent or at fault.

6. The owner of the mare agrees to provide insurance to cover the eventualities described in (5) above.

7. This paragraph gives options if the breeding is not successful, including termination of the breeding contract and a rebreeding to another stallion.

8. The owner of the stallion must agree to provide a breeding certificate to the mare's owner as soon as possible after birth of the foal in order for the mare's owner to register the foal.

9. In the event that one party breaches the contract, the non-breaching party's remedies are set forth, including recovery of attorney's fees if legal action is required.

10. Sets forth the state's law under which any legal action must be taken, and the venue.

13

Breeding Certificate

The breeder (usually the owner of the stallion) should issue a certificate of breeding at the time the mare is returned to its owner after having been bred to the stallion. The certificate should specify the stallion to which the mare was bred and the dates on which the breedings took place. By stating the dates, the mare's owner and the veterinarian can approximate the conception date and the gestation period for the foal, if the mare has been determined to be pregnant, or "in foal."

A particular Registry may not accept an agency appointment. One should check with the Registry in question before naming an appointed agent to sign the breeding certificate if the owner cannot sign the certificate for some reason.

SAMPLE

BREEDING CERTIFICATE

I, _____John Horseman_____ , owner of the stallion named _____March to Time_____ , and described as follows:

Breed: Registration Number 1234567
Description: Dk. Bay, white star on forehead

hereby certify and warrant that said stallion bred the mare named _____Windsong_____ , Registration Number _____7654321_____ and owned by _____Jane Rider_____ which is described as _____liver chestnut, four white socks, stripe on_____ forehead _____ , on the following dates and times:

Date: _____   Time: _____

Date: _____   Time: _____

Date: _____   Time: _____

Date: _____   Time: _____

I hereby agree to execute all necessary registration papers for any foal(s) both of said described breedings and should I fail to do so I appoint [name of agent if allowed by Registry] _____ as my agent who is authorized hereby to execute said necessary papers based on the information set forth herein.

Date: _____ , _____ at _____Morristown, PA._____

John Horseman (Signature)
(Owner of Stallion)

Stableview Farms, Morristown, PA.
(Address)

14

Mare Lease Agreement and Breeding Contract for Mare

In a mare lease agreement, the mare is being leased only for the very specific purpose of breeding. The lessor will remain the owner of the mare, but the lessee will become the sole owner of any foal that is the result of a successful breeding. Normally, and unless specified otherwise in the agreement, the mare is not used for riding, driving or any other such purpose while under the lease agreement. The owner of the mare in turn is relieved of the expenses for the care of the mare for the duration of the lease. The lessee is responsible for providing all costs and expenses for the care and maintenance of the mare for the term of the lease, as well as any additional costs specified under the terms of the lease.

This mare lease agreement should be accompanied by the breeding contract for mare, which spells out specifics of the breeding arrangements for the mare.

MARE LEASE AGREEMENT

THIS AGREEMENT is by and between _____Jane Rider_____ hereinafter referred to as "Lessor" and _____Sandra Jones_____ hereinafter referred to as "Lessee." Lessor hereby leases to Lessee, who is engaged in the business of breeding __Thoroughbred__ horses, the following mare:_____Run for the Money_____ (Name of Mare), a _____Thoroughbred_____ (Breed), for breeding purposes by Lessee.

1. Term of Lease.

The term of this lease shall be for approximately _____one breeding season_____, beginning ___June 1, (year)___ and ending when the foal to be received by Lessee herein has been weaned. Should Lessor leave the mare with Lessee beyond the term of this lease, and/or after at least ten (10) days written notice from Lessee that the mare is ready to be returned to Lessor, then Lessor shall pay the sum of $____15____ per day for feed and board to Lessee, plus necessary veterinary and farrier costs.

2. Lease Payments.

Lessee agrees to pay the Lessor the following sums: $____750____ to be paid when said mare is pronounced in foal; $____750____ on or before __December 1, (year)__. Provided, however, if mare does not come into foal by__September 15, (year)__, Lessee, at his/her/their option, may continue the lease on the same basis in __(year)__ with no additional lease payments over and above those noted above, or he/she/they may terminate this lease and return said mare to Lessor and Lessee shall assume the costs of maintenance to day of termination as agreed to in Paragraph 3.

If the mare is pronounced in foal, but a live foal is not born to said mare for any reason whatsoever, Lessee may, at his/her/their option, renew this lease on the same terms in__(year)__, without additional lease payments, or in the alternative, terminate the lease and all monies paid shall be refunded to Lessee. However, in either case Lessee shall assume the cost of maintenance to date as provided in Paragraph 3. "Live Foal" as used herein shall mean __the foal has stood and nursed from a mare or has been fed by hand, in each case for at least a period of 24 hours.__

3. Care and Maintenance.

As further consideration to Lessor, Lessee promises that he/she/they shall assume the full care and maintenance of Lessor's horse during the term of this lease and agrees to provide reasonable breeding conditions and facilities, furnish proper feed, sufficient water, farrier care, adequate shelter, exercise, medical and veterinary care as required, in a manner consistent with good horse breeding practices in the State of _____ at Lessee's own expense as determined by Lessee. However, should Lessor have received the ten (10) day notice described in paragraph 1, then Lessor shall assume all the costs related to such care.

4. Risk of Loss/Insurance on Mare.

Lessor shall bear all risk of loss from the death or harm to any of its mares unless such loss is caused by the gross negligence of Lessee, its agents or employees, in which case Lessee shall bear such loss. Lessee shall have no responsibility to maintain insurance on the life of the horse during the term of this lease.

5. Liability Insurance.

Lessee shall, at his own expense, at all times during the term of this lease, maintain insurance for injury to or death of persons or loss or damages to their property occurring in or about the premises on which Lessor's horse shall be used for breeding. Such insurance shall provide for $ 500,000 per injury, $ 1,000,000 per accident, and $ 300,000 property damage.

6. Use.

Lessee is authorized to use such mare for breeding purposes only.

7. Sublease/Assignment.

Lessee shall not assign this lease, or any interest herein, nor sublet said mare or in any manner permit the use of Lessor's mare for any purpose other than that which is set forth herein.

8. Indemnity.

Lessee agrees that he will indemnify Lessor against, and hold Lessor and Lessor's horse free and harmless from all liens, encumbrances, charges, and claims whether contractual or imposed by operation of law.

9. Permission to Inspect.

Lessee shall permit the Lessor to inspect the mare at any and all reasonable times after reasonable notice of Lessor's intent to do so.

10. Default.

If either party shall default with respect to any material condition or covenant hereof, by him/her/them to be performed, the other party may, but need not, declare this Agreement to be terminated. The breaching party shall be responsible to the other for reasonable attorney's fees and court costs related to any breach.

11. Waiver.

No delay or omission to exercise any right, power, or remedy accruing to either party on any breach or default of Lessee under this lease shall impair any such right, power, or remedy of said party, nor shall it be construed to be a waiver of any such breach or default, or an acquiescence therein, or in any similar breach or default thereafter occurring; nor shall any waiver of any single breach or default be deemed a waiver of any other breach or default theretofore or thereafter occurring. Any waiver, permit, or approval of any kind or character on the part of either party of any breach or default under this lease, or any waiver on part of the other party of any provision or condition of this lease, must be in writing and should be effective only to extent in such writing specifically set forth. All remedies, either under this lease or by law, or otherwise afforded to Lessor, shall be cumulative and not alternative.

12. Effect of Lease.

The provisions of this lease shall be binding on the heirs, executors, administrators, and assigns of Lessor and Lessee in like manner as on the original parties, unless modified by mutual agreement.

13. (a) Governing Law.

The parties agree that the terms of this lease shall be construed in accordance with and governed by the laws of the State of _____. Any legal action must be brought in _____ (county/municipality).

OR

(b) Arbitration.

The parties to this Agreement mutually agree that any and all disputes arising in connection with this Agreement shall be settled and determined by binding arbitration conducted in accordance with the then existing rules of the American Arbitration Association by one or more arbitrators appointed in accordance with said rules. Said arbitration shall take place in _____ (municipality),_____ (state).

14. Entire Agreement.

This constitutes the entire Agreement between the parties. Any modifications or additions MUST be in writing and signed by all parties to this Agreement. No oral modifications or additions will be considered to be part of this Agreement unless reduced to writing and signed by all parties.

Dated: _____ ,_____

LESSOR: _____   LESSEE: _____

Jane Rider   Sandra Jones
(Name)   (Name)

_____   _____
(Address)   (Address)

Discussion of Mare Lease Agreement

The names of the lessor, lessee, and the mare to be leased are set forth at the beginning of the agreement.

1. Paragraph One sets forth how long the lease will last, and under what conditions it may last longer, and who will bear the costs of the extended stay of mare or mare and foal with the lessee.

2. This is a very important paragraph because (1) it sets forth the schedule when lease payments are to be made; and (2) it describes the parties mutually agreed upon definition of what constitutes a live foal. This definition can vary, but must be mutually agreed upon by the parties and specifically set forth in the agreement.

3. Here the type of care expected to be given the mare (and foal) must be set forth and can be quite specific. This paragraph also delineates who is responsible for the costs and expenses involved in the care and maintenance of the mare and/or foal.

4. The mare owner assumes the risk of injury or loss of the mare and should maintain insurance to cover such loss. The only exception is when the stallion owner or those under his control act with gross negligence in handling and caring for the mare.

5. The risk of liability for the mare causing injury to another person or property shifts to the stallion owner, and he must have insurance to cover such an event.

6. & 7. Unless specified otherwise, the leased mare is not to be ridden, driven, or otherwise used for any purpose than breeding, by the lessee. Neither may the lessee sublet the mare or assign the lease to any other person.

8. This paragraph guarantees the lessor that his/her/their mare will not be subjected to any liens that might be placed on other property in which lessee has an interest.

9. The lessor is allowed reasonable access to inspect the condition of the mare. Specific times and frequencies of inspection may be agreed upon by the parties and set forth here.

10. In case one party does not live up to the terms of the contract, this paragraph describes remedies including who shall pay the attorney's fees for the non-breaching party.

11. This paragraph ensures that any delay or failure to take action on the part of one party does not mean that they have waived their right to do so. For example, it may be that they have delayed taking action in order to give the other party an opportunity to remedy the breach or default, such as providing necessary information, etc.

12. In the event that either party to the lease should die, their heirs and the executors of their estate will be bound by the terms of the lease just as if the deceased party were alive.

13. The parties should agree on which state's law applies to the lease agreement if one of the parties reside in or the lease is entered into in a state other than that in which both the parties reside.
Instead of using the Governing Law clause, you may prefer to use the Arbitration clause, because taking a party to court is very expensive and time-consuming. Arbitration is not cheap, or easy, or speedy either, but it is still quicker and easier than litigation.

Finally the agreement is dated and signed by both parties with their addresses given.

BREEDING CONTRACT FOR MARE

THIS AGREEMENT is made by and between ____John Horseman____ , residing at ____Stableview Road, Westriver, MO____ , hereinafter referred to as "Owner of Mare" and ____Maple Tree Ranch, Inc.____ , a Missouri corporation, located at ____Main St.,____ ____Westriver, MO____ , hereinafter referred to as "Stud Farm."

1. Stallion and Mare.
Stud Farm is the owner of stallion: ____Fancy Feast____ , a ____nine____ -year-old, ____Thoroughbred stallion____ , tattoo # ____1234567____ , and Owner is the owner of the mare named ____Whisk Me Away____ , tattoo # ____9876543____ , described as a ____Thorough-____ ____bred mare____ , foaled in ____(year)____ , by ____Flyaway____ , Reg. No. ____567890____ and, out of ____Whiskbroom____ , due to foal ____March 30, (year)____ .

2. Booking.
____Fancy Feast____ will stand at stud during the ____(date)____ season at Stud Farm, and the parties hereto desire to contract with Owner of Mare for one season's booking from ____September 1, (year), to September 1, (year)____ , for the services of the mare.

3. Fees.
It is agreed as follows:

a. Upon payment of ____five hundred ($500)____ dollars booking fee, which is not refundable, Stud Farm does hereby reserve for the Owner of Mare one season's booking from ____September 1, (year), to September 1, (year)____ , for the services of the mare.

b. (i) The mare shall remain at the Stud Farm for a sufficient time to be pregnancy-checked after having been bred.

(ii) Board at the rate of $____15____ per day for the keeping and ordinary care of the mare and/or foal will be paid by Owner of Mare.

(iii) The balance of the Breeding Fee, $____1,500____ plus all unpaid board and expenses, will be paid when the mare is picked up.

4. Health/Other Requirements.
a. All mares must be accompanied by a health certificate indicating current vaccination for equine influenza (strangles, tetanus, and sleeping sickness are also recommended upon arrival at the Stud Farm). Mares not accompanied by such certificate will be vaccinated shortly after arrival at expense of Owner.

b. Stud Farm requires a negative Coggins Test for Equine Infectious Anemia (Swamp Fever) prior to mare's arrival at Stud Farm.

c. Owner agrees to allow Stud Farm to have a qualified veterinarian check the mare for normal breeding conditions, and to perform such other veterinary services that Stud Farm may deem necessary for the proper treatment and protection of the mare and/or foal at side. Owner is responsible for said services and expense and will be billed and will pay for said services before mare is picked up from Stud Farm.

d. Mares that are not halter broken or cannot be hobbled will not be accepted.

5. Liability.

Stud Farm shall not be liable for any sickness, disease, theft, death, or injury which may be suffered by the mare and/or foal at her side or any other cause of action whatsoever arising out of this breeding contract during the time that the mare is in the custody of Stud Farm except for any acts by the Stud Farm, its officers, agents, contracts, or employees that amount to gross negligence. Owner fully understands that Stud Farm does not carry any outside insurance on horse(s) that are in their possession for breeding and boarding of the mare or mares.

6. Insurance.

Owner of Mare shall maintain at his own expense insurance for injury to or death of persons or loss or damage to their property occurring in or about the premises of the Stud Farm for the term of this Agreement. Such insurance shall provide $ __500,000__ per injury, $ __1,000,000__ per accident, and $ __300,000__ for property damage. Owner must provide proof of such insurance.

7. Return Breeding.

Stud Farm guarantees a return breeding the following season provided the stallion is able to service mares either for said mare or an approved substitute should a live foal not result from this mating. For the purposes of this Agreement, a live foal shall be one that stands and nurses without assistance. This is to be evidenced by a written statement from a qualified veterinarian. In the event the stallion is not able to re-service said mare, Stud Farm may substitute another stallion at Owner of Mare's option or all monies paid by Owner of Mare for the previous service, not including expenses, shall be refunded to Owner of Mare.

8. Assignment.

This contract shall not be assigned or transferred by either party hereto without the consent of the other. If the mare is to be rebred and Owner of Mare fails to deliver her for breeding the following year, then any and all fees paid shall not be refundable and this contract is thereby canceled.

9. (a) Governing Law.

This Agreement shall be governed by and in accordance with the laws of the State of __Missouri_____ . Any legal action must be brought in _____ (county/municipality).

OR

(b) Arbitration.

The parties to this Agreement mutually agree that any and all disputes arising in connection with this Agreement shall be settled and determined by binding arbitration conducted in accordance with the then existing rules of the American Arbitration Association by one or more arbitrators appointed in accordance with said rules. Said arbitration shall take place in_____ (municipality),_____ (state).

10. Entire Agreement.

This constitutes the entire Agreement between the parties. Any modifications or additions MUST be in writing and signed by all parties to this Agreement. No oral modifications or additions will be considered to be part of this Agreement unless reduced to writing and signed by all parties.

Dated _____

Stud Farm Owner   Owner of Mare

_____   _____
Maple Tree Ranch, Inc.,   John Horseman
a Missouri corporation

Discussion of Breeding Contract for Mare

The name of the owner of the mare and the name of the stud farm and its location are set forth at the beginning of the document.

1. The mare's description and identification is set forth here. The Mare Information Form should also accompany this agreement.

2. The stallion that the mare is to be bred to is described here.

3. The amount of the stud fees and the payment schedule is specifically set forth here.

4. The stringent health and behavior requirements of the Stud Farm are set forth here.

5. This is the "hold harmless" clause in the agreement. This limit on liability would only apply to ordinary negligence. The Stud Farm would still be liable if there was gross negligence on the part of the Stud Farm or anyone under its control.

6. The mare owner remains responsible if anyone or anyone's property is injured or lost due to something the mare did while at the Stud Farm. The Stud Farm would require the mare owner to carry a minimum amount of insurance to cover these events should they occur and should demand proof of such insurance.

7. This paragraph guarantees a rebreeding if a live foal does not result from the breeding. It is imperative that the parties agree on a clear definition of "live foal" and place that definition in this paragraph.

8. Neither party may assign their interest in this contract to third party without the consent of the other party. This also covers what will happen as to the return of fees in the event that a rebreeding is scheduled but the owner fails to bring the mare to the Stud Farm.

9. This paragraph sets forth which state's law applies in the event of any legal action, and the venue for any legal action.

15

Mare Information Form

The Mare Information Form should be completed and accompany the mare when she is delivered to be bred.

MARE INFORMATION FORM

Booked to ___Fairhaven Ranch___ (Name of Stallion's Farm)

Owner's Name: ___George Williams___
Phone No.: ___(555) 555-5555___
Address: ___101 West Main Street___
___Anytown, KS___

Mare's Name: ___Winsome Miss___
Tattoo No. ___123456___

___Sir Hoover___
(Sire's Sire)

___Hoover Dam___
(Sire)

___Gulfstream Girl___
(Sire's Dam)

___Winsome Miss___
(Mare)

___Hardy Boy___
(Dam's Sire)

___Miss Daisy___
(Dam)

___Daisy Field___
(Dam's Dam)

Foaled: ___1988___ Color: ___Chestnut___

Markings: ___Left hind sock; blaze on forehead___

Anticipated arrival date at stud farm: ___May 1, (year)___

Foal at side: ___No___ Sire of Foal: ___N/A___

Date of last foaling: ___April 14, (year)___

Mare to remain at breeding farm until pregnancy check? Yes _X_ No ___

Does Mare have any dangerous propensities? If yes, describe below.

    Tends to turn hindquarters to anyone entering stall and will
    sometimes kick out at strangers doing so.

Reproductive History of Mare:

    Five normal pregnancies; one with assisted
    birth; five live foals.

Breeding History:

Date of last breeding: _March, (year)_ Problems, if any: _Did not conceive._

Medications: _None_

Hormones (F.S.H., L.H., Progesterone), if used: _None_

Other: _____

Vaccination History:

Tetanus Toxois:_____Yes_____ Date: _January (year)_

VEE: _February (year)_

Encephalomyelitis (sleeping sickness),
Eastern & Western strains: _January (year)_

Coggins: _____

Date of last worming: _April (year)_

Colic: _Yes_ Frequency: _One mild episode, April (year)_

Founder: _No_ When: _N/A_

Allergies, if known: _None_

Other: _____

Feeding Program:

Hay type: _Orchard grass; alfalfa_ Amount: _4 flakes per day_

Grain type/s: _Sweet feed/alfalfa cubes_ Amount: _1/2 lb. per feeding_

Pellets:_____   Amount:_____

Known Allergies to feeds: <u>None</u>

Special Care Requirement: <u>None</u>

_____

_____

_____

Habits: <u>Slow eater, will leave some feed until next feeding, but ulti-
mately consumes all.</u>

Whom to contact in case of emergency, if owner cannot be reached:

Willow Creek Veterinary Hospital, 24-hour emergency service.
Tel. (555) 555-5555

Is the mare insured? Yes ___X___ No_____

<u>Equine Insurers Group   (444) 444-4444</u>
Name of Insurance Company   Telephone No.

<u>1111 Horse Lane, Southriver, IL</u>
Address

<u>$10,000</u>
Amount of Insurance

<u>Jeff Nelson</u>
Insurance Agent

16

Boarding Agreement

When owners keep a horse or horses on someone else's property, they are boarding the horse. A boarding agreement covers the rights and responsibilities of the horse owner and of the stable or farm where the horse is boarded. Board may range from a simple turn out agreement with the owner providing all the food and care to a full service facility.

The need for a formal boarding agreement becomes clear when you consider the following situations.

In one true case, the owner believed she was boarding her pony in exchange for allowing the pony to be used in the lesson program. The agreement was entirely verbal. After ten months, the parties had widely divergent interpretations of the agreement. The stable declared it owned the pony, based on board that was past due. The owner hired a lawyer to regain control of her pony, but, in the meantime, the stable had sold the pony. After a year, the owner received a $500 judgment, but never saw the pony again.

In another instance, an owner loaned his horse to a high school girl who boarded it at a nearby stable, but she did not pay her board bills. At the end of the winter, when the owner called to ask for the horse back, he learned he must pay $3,500 in back board or lose his horse to the boarding stable. He did not have $3,500, so he lost his horse.

Example: Jane, after years of riding lessons, decides to take the big step into horse ownership and buys a horse. She lives in the city and commutes to the boarding stable where she takes lessons. She pays $5,000 for her horse, a nonregistered Thoroughbred. Because she cannot be at the stable daily, Jane wants her horse exercised regularly, and she needs special services: grooming, blanketing, and tack-up to save her time. She also wants her horse turned out daily, but with only one other horse at a time. Finally, her horse loses weight easily and needs a specific feeding schedule.

Some stables have a standard boarding contract that outlines the responsibilities of the stable and the owner. In this case, Jane needs to provide her own contract. The following is Jane's agreement.

SAMPLE

BOARDING AGREEMENT

This Agreement is made _____ July 10, (year) _____ , between Oak Cottage Stable (referred to as "Stable") located at _745 Fireplace Road, Southriver, New York_ and _Jane Rider_ (referred to as "Owner") residing at _133 West Main Street, New York, New York_ , owner of the horse described in Section 2.

1. Fees.

(a) In consideration of _five hundred and fifty ($ 550.00)_ Dollars per horse per month paid by Owner in advance on the first day of each month, the stable agrees to board said horse beginning _August 1, (year)_ .

(b) Options to the basic fee paid in the same timely fashion are available as listed below. Each additional requested service must be circled and initialed by the owner. These options can be changed at any time Stable receives written notice from Owner. The fees are subject to change given ___30___ days written notice by Stable.

(1)	Exercise fee	- $ 80.00
(2)	Blanketing when appropriate (owner provides the blanket)	- $ 15.00
(3)	Supplemental vitamins for coat and hoof protein	- $ 15.00
(4)	Daily grooming	- $ 25.00
(5)	Tack-up service with three hours notice	- $ 25.00
(6)	General Supplies	- $ 25.00

2. Description of the Horse(s).

Name:	Lucky Break
Age:	10 years
Color:	Bay
Sex:	Gelding
Breed:	Unknown, t.b. type
Height:	16 hands
Registration/Tatoo No.:	None

3. Turn-Out.

If no options are chosen, the Owner will be expressly responsible for all exercise, and it is understood that the horse will (will not) be turned out.

4. Standard of Care.

All care is provided by Owner.

OR

Stable agrees to provide normal and reasonable care to maintain the health and well-being of said horse.

Optional Special Instructions:

(a) Box stall sized 10' by 12'.

(b) Daily turn-out with no more than one other horse.

(c) 10 quarts of sweet feed grain — 10%.

(d) Hay in stall at all times (alfalfa/timothy mix).

5. Risk of Loss/Hold Harmless.

[Add here Release and Hold Harmless clause in accordance with and using the language of the state in which the Agreement is made, if that state has passed an Equine Activity Liability Law.]

[If your state has not passed such a law, use the following clause: "Lessee agrees to hold Lessor harmless from any act of ordinary negligence of Lessor or any of his agents, contractors, or employees arising from any accident, injury, or damage whatsoever, however caused, to any person or persons, or the property of any person, persons, or corporations occurring during such term of this Lease and arising out of the use or care of said horse."]

6. Indemnity.

Owner agrees to hold Stable harmless from any claim caused by said horse(s) and agrees to pay legal fees incurred by Stable in defense of a claim resulting from damage by said horse(s).

7. Emergency Care.

If medical treatment is needed, Stable will call Owner. In the event Owner is not reached, Stable has the authority to secure emergency veterinary and/or blacksmith care. However, Stable has no responsibility to pay for such emergency care. Owner is responsible to pay all costs relating to this care. Stable is authorized to arrange billing to the Owner, but Owner must make such arrangements with veterinarian and clinic in advance.

8. Shoeing and Worming.

Stable agrees to implement a shoeing and worming program, consistent with recognized standards. Owner is obligated to pay the expenses of such services, including a reasonable stable charge. Such bill shall be paid within fifteen days from the date the bill is submitted to Owner.

9. Ownership - Coggins Test.

Owner warrants that he owns the horse and will provide, prior to the time of delivery, proof of a negative Coggins test.

10. Termination.

Either party may terminate this Agreement. In the event of a default, the wronged party has the right to recover attorneys' fees and court costs, resulting from this failure of either party to meet a material term of this Agreement.

11. Notice.

Owner agrees to give Stable thirty (30) days notice to terminate this Agreement. The Owner cannot assign this Agreement unless the Stable agrees in writing.

12. Right of Lien.

Stable has the right of lien as set forth in the law of the State of ___New York___ for the amount due for board and additional agreed upon services and shall have the right, without process of law, to retain said horse(s) until the indebtedness is satisfactorily paid in full.

13. (a) Governing Law.

This Agreement is subject to the laws of the State of ___New York___. Any legal action must be taken in _____(county/municipality). The parties have executed this Agreement this _____day of _____ , (year).

OR

(b) Arbitration.

The parties to this Agreement mutually agree that any and all disputes arising in connection with this Agreement shall be settled and determined by binding arbitration conducted in accordance with the then existing rules of the American Arbitration Association by one or more arbitrators appointed in accordance with said rules. Said arbitration shall take place in _____ (municipality), _____ (state).

14. Entire Agreement.

This constitutes the entire Agreement between the parties. Any modifications or additions MUST be in writing and signed by all parties to this Agreement. No oral modifications or additions will be considered to be part of this Agreement unless reduced to writing and signed by all parties.

STABLE:

Signed by: _____

_____

Address

_____

Telephone

OWNER:

Signed by: _____

_____

Address

_____

Telephone

Discussion

In the opening statement, the agreement is dated and the parties are identified. If the stable is incorporated, its title will be followed by <u>"Inc., a corporation of the State of</u>
<u>   </u> with its principal place of business located<u>   </u>."
The form also provides additional blank space to include the corporate wording where applicable.

1. (a) The basic fee is stated, indicating the monthly board and the due date for accounts receivable. Sometimes the owner receives a reduced rate in exchange for sharing the horse with the stable for lessons. This modified rate can be clarified here. The date the board actually begins is important because the horse's arrival often does not coincide with the date on the contract. Jane may have signed the agreement on one day, but may not have had her horse delivered for two more weeks.

    (b) Overhead in the horse business is very high. Few people recognize the true costs involved in feeding and caring for horses with rising costs for grain, hay, and bedding in a labor-intense business. Stables are advised to collect whatever fees (basic board and additional services) possible at the beginning of each month before the horse moves in. Otherwise, the stable is carrying the boarder for thirty days on its own credit.

Too often owners are not clear on the services provided and are angry if they think they are not getting their money's worth. This section, stating the extra services and fees, can save much bitterness after the board has begun and the cost of the total board varies to reflect the actual services offered.

Here the stable describes precisely its additional services and fees. These have been filled in on the sample form but may remain blank if none of these services is provided, or they may be listed with no charge following each item to indicate they are automatically included in the board. In addition, a general supplies charge may be added here to cover the fly spray and saddle soap that is often treated as community property anyway. This charge may also include a laundry fee for pads and bandages.

2. The horse or horses boarded by the owner are described.

3. The turn-out policy is best stated separately. Some stables provide turn-out only and the owner assumes all care of the horse. With the price of land skyrocketing in certain prime locations within commuting distance of large urban areas, it is not uncommon to find a relatively large stable on a small piece of property. Horses may be turned out in large groups or individually for short periods. This policy needs to be clearly established.

4. All care may be provided by the owner, often called rough board, and the boarding rate is greatly reduced, or, at the other end of the scale, the owner may clarify instruction as to quantity and quality of feed. The stable may specify what the horse will be fed under the boarding fee as stated and may collect additional fees for extras like bedding.

The owner should be familiar with the care provided by the chosen stable and be certain that it is adequate. If he/she is not experienced in determining this, a professional should be asked to advise.

On the other hand, stables should be aware that owners who insist on feed and schedules not consistent with barn routine and practices may create havoc in a stable feed room. Nevertheless, most stables welcome requests that assist them in maintaining the new boarder's health.

5. This section is imperative because of the high price of stable insurance these days. If your state is one that has enacted an Equine Activity Liability Law, you must use the precise lan-

guage the law requires and the exact size or type required. Some stables require all boarders to be insured, but at very least, liability for loss of the horse must be clearly placed on the owner's shoulders, barring clear malfeasance of the stable or its employees.

6. If the owner's horse injures someone and that person sues the stable, the owner will indemnify (repay) the stable for its costs defending the claim.

7. This clause is meant to protect the horse. For example, if the horse falls and rips open his knee on a stone while the owner is on vacation, the stable is authorized to call the vet to administer emergency care and have the owner billed directly.

The owner, however, should leave a copy of the horse's insurance policy with the stable manager if the policy dictates that a particular procedure be followed before any surgical process is undertaken. The name and telephone number of a preferred vet should also be available to the stable. Stables are advised to contact the owner before deciding on any optional care beyond the immediate need for saving the horse's life. The owner cannot expect the stable to pay for such emergency care because it can sometimes amount to thousands of dollars. Therefore, the owner should get the veterinarian and clinic to agree to accept the owner's credit in the event such emergency care is required and the owner cannot be located.

8. This is the policy for shoeing and worming. Generally, all worming is done at the same time in a barn and both services are most efficiently handled in the barn.

The stables, however, should avoid fronting costs for these services. Direct billing is preferable or the stable can invoke a service charge included for the time and effort.

9. The owner, Jane, warrants she owns the horse and she must show proof of a negative Coggins test. The Coggins test is widely used to test for a dangerous, usually fatal, contagious disease. This ownership requirement eliminates a situation where the person boarding the horse may not own it and fails to pay the boarding bill.

10. This allows the stable or the owner to break the agreement and recover the costs of damages if one side does not abide by the contract. The owner has paid in advance, and he is entitled to have a percentage of his fee returned if he must move his horse because the care of the horse is not as agreed. If he must hire a lawyer to collect, he can sue the stable for reasonable costs. Nevertheless, as in all contracts, the parties should try to mediate, because these court cases can be difficult and time consuming to resolve.

11. The owner is required to give the stable thirty days notice before breaking the agreement. A stable usually orders feed and hires help according to its bookings. One horse leaving a stable is usually not a problem, but some owners may own a significant number of horses and it would disrupt a stable if they all left at once. In addition, the stable may have a waiting list and needs time to notify new boarders.

12. This clause provides security for the stable that bills will be paid. The owner may not move the horse until the bill is paid and, under extreme circumstances, and with written notice, and according to the laws of the particular state, the stable could sell the horse or take over ownership to recoup the unpaid bill.

13. & 14. Different states have different laws and some stables have several locations. The agreement is subject to the laws of the state named in the agreement. The venue where any legal action would be taken is also named or the parties may select an arbitration clause. The date the agreement is signed appears next with the stable signature by an authorized agent and the owner's signature, with respective addresses and telephones.

17

Training Agreement

A training agreement is a contract between a trainer and a horse owner. The trainer is paid for schooling a horse over a specified period. The training agreement **may** also include boarding the horse at the trainer's stable, and in this case, the cost of the board and the training fees are itemized separately.

Training agreements can be complicated and do require written contracts. For instance, when an owner makes an agreement with a trainer, the trainer may receive part ownership of a horse in exchange for publicizing the owner's stable. In one case, a rider contended she was asked by the stable owner to train at his stable for one year in return for part ownership of a horse, yet to be purchased, within a certain price range. They agreed with a handshake that the rider would train and show horses to promote the farm and attract boarders. Later, the owner alleged he had only promised a ten percent ownership in the horse per year as an incentive. In the interim, the horse was purchased and the horse's value increased dramatically. Each party believed he owned the horse. The original contract terms had been verbal and were in complete dispute. After failed mediation, the case landed in court, and the three-week trail ended in a decision in favor of the trainer. The court ruled that the trainer owned the horse under the agreement and the stable owner would receive compensation for the six months the trainer had left to fulfill the contract.

Example: Owner Linda Barnes purchases a green horse, Sky Pilot, to be trained by Nancy Rider. Linda wants her horse schooled and shown. Eventually, she hopes to show the horse as an adult hunter the following season. Linda has several concerns about the training agreement. She has heard stories of training bills with other trainers that have become excessive and worries that there will be many unforeseen extra expenses attached to the monthly bills. She also wonders whether she should carry liability or mortality insurance.

Furthermore, Linda feels she should get a reduction in the training fee if the horse is lame or injured over an extended period. She also wants a clause relating to the winning of prize money, although in many situations this would not apply. Finally she does not want to be committed to a long-term agreement. The following contract should suit her.

97

TRAINING AGREEMENT

THIS TRAINING AGREEMENT (the "Agreement") made this _____ day of _____ _____ (year) , by and between: _____Linda Barnes_____ , hereinafter referred to as "Owner," and _____Nancy Rider_____ and _____Oak Cottage Stable_____ , hereinafter referred to as "Trainer."

    WITNESSETH that Owner owns the below described horse(s) and covenants with Trainer to train said horse(s) for the purpose and under the terms hereto agreed as follows:

1. Description of Horse and Delivery.

Trainer agrees to arrange transportation to _____Oak Cottage Stable_____ on or about_____July 7, (year)_____ at Owner's expense the following described horse(s):

Name of Horse	Age	Color	Sex	Breed
1. Sky Pilot	5 years	ch.	gelding	Morgan
2.				
3.				
4.				

2. Training Fee and Terms of Payment.

Owner shall pay a fee of _____Forty_____ Dollars ($___40.00___) per day per horse, payable as follows:

    (a) Each payment to be due and payable by the first of each month.

    (b) Any payment not received by the seventh of each month shall incur interest at 12% per annum for the number of days past the first.

    (c) Payment not received by the fifteenth of each month is subject to a $15.00 penalty charge over and above the monthly bill.

3. Additional Expenses.

    Owner shall be responsible for all costs directly related to this Agreement, including but not limited to transportation, veterinary bills, entries, grooming fees, and necessary special equipment. Owner will not be responsible for additional expenses exceeding_____One Thousand_____Dollars ($_1,000.00_) per month without prior written approval. All additional expenses are due and payable on the first of the month as provided by Section 2.

4. Trainer Responsibilities.

    (a) Trainer shall fulfill the duties in a manner consistent with good show training practices in this County of _____ in the State of _____ :

    1. to maintain the health and well-being of the horse at a level of fitness necessary for light showing.

    2. to school the horse on the flat and over fences to the point at which the horse can perform a three (3) foot hunter course at a show with flying changes.

(b) Trainer shall pay all expenses according to Section 2, sending Owner an accounting each month.

In the event Trainer is not reimbursed on time, Trainer is authorized to deduct said payments from any other source available to Trainer.

(c) Trainer shall obtain all necessary veterinary and farrier services and as agent may authorize direct billing to the Owner. Any extraordinary care over and beyond normal and regular maintenance requires prior written approval by Owner unless involving the most immediate emergency treatment.

5. Showing.

(a) Any prize money won by Owner's horse while under this Agreement shall be treated as follows:

1. Trainer receives 50% of said prize money as a bonus.

2. The remaining 50% of said prize money shall be credited to Owner's account.

(b) Owner's horse(s) shall be shown in name of _____ Sky Pilot _____ with Linda Barnes _____ as Owner and _____ Nancy Rider _____ as Trainer.

6. Lay-ups.

If said horse(s) is out of training for more than _____ seven _____ days consecutively, Owner shall pay the cost of board at _____ Thirty _____ Dollars ($ 30.00) per day plus incidental expenses as required. Owner must be notified within _____ five _____ (5) days if horse is taken out of training.

7. Term and Termination.

(a) The term of this Agreement shall be _____ on a month to month _____ basis. Either party may terminate Agreement given _____ three _____ (3) days written notice, provided a final accounting by the Trainer is presented and all payments have been made by Owner prior to taking possession of said horse(s).

(b) On termination, Trainer shall have a lien on said horse(s) under _____ Maryland _____ law for all unpaid charges on account. Payment must be made in full before said horse(s) is released unless Trainer consents in writing.

8. Insurance.

(a) Owner shall bear all risk of loss from the death of or any harm to said horse(s) unless such loss is caused by gross negligence of Trainer, his agents, contractors, or employees, in which case Trainer shall bear such loss.

(b) Trainer agrees/does not agree to carry insurance protecting Owner against any losses caused by negligence of Trainer, his agents and employees.

(c) Owner agrees to reimburse Trainer _____% of the premium for said insurance.

(d) Trainer agrees/does not agree to maintain liability insurance.

1. $_____ per person
2. $_____ per accident
3. $_____ property damage

If insurance is so provided, Trainer will make a copy of the policy available to Owner.

9. Indemnification.

Owner agrees to indemnify Trainer unless otherwise provided by insurance against all liability or claims, demands, and costs for or arising out of this Agreement unless such are caused by the gross negligence of Trainer, his agents, contractors, or employees.

10. Binding Effect.

(a) The parties hereto agree that this Agreement shall be binding on their respective heirs, successors, and assigns.

(b) Failure of either party to abide by and perform any and all other terms, covenants, conditions, and obligations of this Agreement shall constitute a default and shall, in addition to any other remedies provided by law or in equity, entitle the wronged party to reasonable attorneys' fees and court costs related to such breach.

11. (a) Governing Law.

This Agreement shall be governed by and in accordance with the laws of the State of_____
_____ . Any legal action must be brought in _____
(county/municipality).

OR

(b) Arbitration.

The parties to this Agreement mutually agree that any and all disputes arising in connection with this Agreement will be settled and determined by binding arbitration conducted in accordance with the then existing rules of the American Arbitration Association by one or more arbitrators appointed in accordance with said rules. Said arbitration shall take place in _____
(municipality), _____ (state).

12. Entire Agreement.

This constitutes the entire Agreement between the parties. Any modifications or additions MUST be in writing and signed by all parties to this Agreement. No oral modifications or additions will be considered to be part of this Agreement unless reduced to writing and signed by all parties.

IN WITNESS WHEREOF, the parties have executed this Agreement on the day and year first above written.

OWNER: TRAINER:

_____   _____
Signature   Signature

_____   _____
Address   Address

_____   _____

_____   _____
Telephone   Telephone

Discussion

First, the training agreement sets the date of the agreement and names the owner, stable, and trainer. The general purpose is stated, and it is established that the owner owns the horse and desires the trainer to school the horse, and the trainer has consented.

1. The trainer arranges the delivery of the horse at the expense of the owner. The horse or horses are described.

2. The terms of payment are set out on a per diem cost basis. Bills are due on the first of the month and late payments are subject to an interest charge, set by the parties to the contract. If payment is not received by the fifteenth of each month, there is an additional $15 handling fee. These figures are arbitrary, but should not be usurious. Nevertheless, stringent rules are needed to encourage timely payment because of the high overhead of the business.

3. The owner is responsible for all additional expenses, including veterinary charges, show-related costs, and the purchase of training equipment. If the incidental costs exceed a specific amount, prior approval is required. Costs mount quickly and this clause enables the owner to control additional expenses. On the other hand, the trainer may have paid for some charges out of pocket and needs to be assured of reimbursement.

4. The trainer's duties are clarified. The basic standard of care is described, followed by any specific responsibilities.
- **(a)** The owner should know the trainer and personally examine his operation before entrusting the horse to him. Professional advice is helpful and references provide added reassurance. For instance, the owner should determine if the trainer's horses are healthy and happy looking and are consistent winners. This contract states the owner's expectations in terms of the schooling and showing level.
- **(b)** The trainer must send a monthly accounting of expenses and is authorized to deduct any unpaid balance from the owner's account.
- **(c)** The trainer organizes the regular maintenance of vaccinations, worming, shoeing, and other medical requirements. He is authorized to arrange direct billing. Any medical expenses over and beyond the customary regular maintenance require prior approval unless they involve emergency treatment, and even then the trainer is not required to make any out-of-pocket expenditures.

5. The allocation of prize money is optional. Some owners keep 100% of the money, but usually the trainer and owner split the prize money. This section also clarifies the horse's show name and the ownership for show purposes. This prevents a trainer from showing a client's horse under his own name.

6. Linda was concerned that her horse might go lame or be taken out of training for some other purpose. Under the terms of this section, she will be notified when her horse is not in work and charged a reduced rate.

7. The term of this agreement can be any length. Here it is on a month-to-month basis, as Linda prefers. A contract like this is rarely more than a year with the ability to renew. Either side may end the agreement with three days' written notice, but the owner cannot take the horse off the premises without settling the bill. The trainer has a lien on the horse under state law and can, under the worst case scenario, sell the horse at auction to settle the account. For this reason, trainers are advised to keep accounts current; there can be times when the horse is not worth the bill, and the owner is broke.

8. Insurance is optional, but recommended, because it protects all parties, especially the owner who must bear the loss if the horse is injured or dies.

In addition, this clause releases the trainer and his agents from all liability unless there is gross negligence. Many contracts release them from all liability, including any level of negligence. This is a negotiable point. Trainers are well advised to carry liability insurance in the event a horse injures someone on their property, and the owner will often require this safeguard and be willing to pay a part of the premium.

9. In the event there is no insurance or a claim exceeds the insurance, the owner will reimburse the trainer for any claims relating to the owner's horse.

10. (a) The agreement binds all succeeding parties in case the original person dies or a subsequent person is assigned in his place; for example, if a parent assigns ownership of the horse to a relative.
   (b) The person who breaks the terms of the agreement will be responsible for all reasonable legal fees if there are attorney or court costs.
   (c) The laws of one resident state are chosen to govern, and the venue for any legal action is named. Alternatively, the parties to the agreement may choose the arbitration clause.

11. Too often the parties start altering the terms of a contract verbally and this can lead to confusion and conflict later. Any alterations in the agreement must be added in writing.

Finally, both parties execute the agreement by signing it.

18

Training Agreement for Racehorse

An agreement for training racehorses is very similar to the previous training agreement, but it must cover details of who will pay the costs involved in racing. The division of the purse money must also be described precisely.

TRAINING AGREEMENT FOR RACEHORSE

THIS AGREEMENT is made on _____July 25, (year)_____ between _Singing Hills Ranch, a California corporation_____, located at _1234 Special Road, Winners, California,_____ herein called "Owner," and _____John Horseman_____ residing at _____Bridge Street, San Diego,_____ _California_____, herein called "Trainer."

   Owner is the legal owner of certain thoroughbred horses described below bred for racing and is desirous of having these horses trained and raced. Trainer is a Thoroughbred racehorse trainer and desirous of training and racing these horses.

   In consideration of the promises and agreements herein set forth, the parties agree as follows:

1. Description/Delivery of Horses.

   Owner agrees to deliver the following horses to trainer to be trained and raced at_____ _Del Mar Race Track_____ (or at racetracks throughout the State of _California_____ as the case may be):

Name of Horse	Age	Color & Sex	Jockey Club Registration No.
Tommy's Triumph	2	Bay/Colt	568943
Top Gun	3	Chestnut/Colt	478921

2. Training Fees.

   a. Owner agrees to pay Trainer_____ Dollars per day per horses trained and /or raced, subject to the provisions of Section 6. This daily charge shall be payable on or before the _fifteenth_____ day of each month.

   b. In the event that any of Owner's horses win a race, Owner shall allocate ten (10) percent from Owner's share of the purse money and said ten percent shall be paid to Trainer over and above any compensation as set forth in **(a)** above.

   c. In addition, Owner shall deduct another ten (10) percent from such purse money to be paid to the jockey riding the Owner's horse in the winning race.

   d. No deductions shall be made nor any monies paid to Trainer or the jockey from purse money received by the Owner as compensation for Owner's horse finishing in any other position than the winning position.

3. Duties of Trainer.

   Trainer shall train and race the horses and feed and care for them, subject to Section 4 herein, in a manner consistent with accepted horse training practices in the State of_____California_____. Trainer, in his sole discretion, shall decide when any of Owner's horses are sufficiently trained to be entered in a race, and Trainer has sole discretion to decide what type of race any horse may be entered in and how often each horse should be raced, except that Trainer shall not enter any of Owner's horses in any claiming race for the sum of $_____Dollars or less without prior consent of Owner.

4. Expenses.

Owner shall bear the cost of transporting the horses from one track to another or otherwise, veterinary and medical costs, costs of preparation of racing silks, jockey fees, pony leads, and/or any costs of equipment that Trainer may deem necessary to the proper training and racing of any of Owner's horses, in addition to insurance costs as set forth in Section 8 below.

5. Accounting and Billing by Trainer.

Trainer shall pay all expenses referred to in Section 4, keep an accurate account thereof, and bill Owner for the same at the end of each month. If Owner fails to reimburse Trainer for such expenses when payable, Trainer is authorized to deduct an amount equal to such expenses from Owner's account from the Horsemen's Bookkeeper at the race track where Owner's horses are being trained and raced, pursuant to the limited power of attorney set forth in connection with this Agreement and incorporated herein by reference.

6. Horses Out of Training.

If, during the term of this Agreement, any of Owner's horses are taken out of training after being put into training, Owner shall pay the costs of boarding, feeding, veterinarian services and medicine, and transportation in maintaining any such horse, but shall not pay Trainer compensation for training as hereinabove set forth. Trainer shall notify Owner as soon as it is known that horse is or has been removed from training, and Owner shall pay thereafter $_____Dollars per day until the horse can be returned to training or can no longer remain at the track.

7. Amendment/Additions.

This Agreement may be amended at any time by writing into the provisions herein set forth the description of any additional racing stock desired by both parties to be placed within the terms of this Agreement, and the amendment shall be initialed by both parties.

8. Insurance and Indemnification.

a) **Insurance**. Upon receipt of the horses herein described, Trainer shall procure Thoroughbred racehorse insurance protecting Owner against any losses due to fire, theft, death, or other disability arising from any injuries of accidents to said horses, such insurance to provide coverage in an amount not less than $_____Dollars. Owner agrees to reimburse Trainer for such insurance costs in the manner set forth in Section 5 above.

b) **Indemnification**. Trainer agrees to indemnify Owner from all liability or claims, demands, damages, and costs for or arising out of the training and racing of Owner's horses, whether it be caused by the negligence of Trainer, his agents, contractors, employees, or otherwise.

9. Termination.

If this Agreement is terminated for any reason prior to the expiration thereof, Trainer shall immediately deliver any horses under this Agreement to Owner at Owner's/Trainer's expense.

10. (a) Governing Law.

This Agreement shall be governed by and in accordance with the laws of the State of _____.
Any legal action must be brought in _____ (county/municipality).

OR

(b) Arbitration.

The parties to this Agreement mutually agree that any and all disputes arising in connection with this Agreement shall be settled and determined by binding arbitration conducted in accordance with the then existing rules of the American Arbitration Association by one or more arbitrators appointed in accordance with said rules. Said arbitration shall take place in _____ (municipality), _____ (state).

11. Entire Agreement.

This constitutes the entire Agreement between the parties. Any modifications or additions MUST be in writing and signed by all parties to this Agreement. No oral modifications or additions will be considered to be part of this Agreement unless reduced to writing and signed by all parties.

DATED: _____

_____   _____
(Name - Owner)   (Name - Trainer)

_____   _____
(Address)   (Address)

_____   _____

Discussion

The agreement begins with the names and addresses of the owner and the trainer and describes generally the purpose of the agreement.

1. The horses to be trained under the agreement are described and identified here.

2. The amount and schedule of payment of training fees and other compensation are set forth in detail here, including jockey's winning fees.

3. The extent of the duties and responsibilities of the trainer are described here.

4. Expenses to be borne by the owner are set forth in detail in this paragraph.

5. Billing and accounting responsibilities are described here. **A limited power of attorney signed by the owner should accompany this agreement.**

6. This paragraph controls what happens in the event a horse is taken out of training for whatever reason.

7. The agreement may be amended and new horses added as long as any amendment or addition is initialed by both parties. This point is reinforced in Section 11.

8. This paragraph sets forth who has responsibility for procuring and maintaining insurance and who will indemnify whom in case of loss or liability.

9. If the agreement is terminated, the trainer must immediately return to owner all owner's horses.

10. A particular state is designated in the event of need for legal action, or the parties choose an arbitration clause.

19

Lease of Boarding and Training Facility

Sometimes a trainer or instructor will wish to lease an existing facility (rather than purchasing a property) to establish a training center for his clients' horses or to provide a place for lessons and for his students' horses and possibly some lesson horses to be boarded.

The lease agreement should carefully address **all** the facilities to be leased, such as a riding arena, office, even toilet facilities, etc., rather than just naming the farm, stable, or ranch in the lease agreement. The owner may wish to retain use of a part of the facility; if this is the case, then there must be a clear delineation of each party's rights and obligations to the other.

Often, if the lessee is only leasing a part of a facility, he may want to contract with the lessor (owner) to have the horses fed and the stalls and/or paddocks cleaned by the same persons who take care of the lessor's horses. A sample agreement, a feed and stall cleaning contract, is attached as optional to the lease agreement. The critical issue for the lessee is that if the lessor's employees do the work, they must be established to be independent contractors and **not** employees of the lessee. Otherwise, the lessee may be liable for the employee's negligence or may have to carry workman's compensation insurance and be responsible for the tax withholdings for the employee.

If the lessee does not wish to lease the entire facility initially, but may wish to do so later on, there is an option provision in the lease agreement. The lessor probably will insist that the lessee maintain liability insurance to relieve the lessor of liability in the event that a person or property is injured or damaged as a result of an activity involving the lessee.

SAMPLE

LEASE OF BOARDING AND TRAINING FACILITY

1. Parties.
THIS AGREEMENT is entered into between _____John and Jane Horseman,_____ dba Hilltop Stables _____, hereinafter referred to as "LESSORS," and Robert and Susan Rider _____, hereinafter referred to as "LESSEES."

2. Subject of Lease.
The property to be leased consists of the ___thirty___ (__30__)-stall barn, acreage, and facilities commonly known as_____Hilltop Stables_____ located at Hilltop Road, Lexington, CT _____ .
The property, as described above, also includes, but is not limited to___two outdoor___ riding arenas, one indoor riding arena, three turnout pastures, one hot-walker, one wash-stall, one office, and one pay telephone (include all fixtures, etc.,) all of which are to be contained within the terms of this lease Agreement.

3. Terms of Lease.
This lease shall commence on _____August 1, (year)_____ and terminate on August 1, (year) _____ , for a period of ___12___ months. At the end of the first term, the LESSEES have the option to renew the lease for the further period of twelve (12) months by advising LESSORS in writing at any time prior to ninety (90) days prior to the expiration of this lease. A yearly cost of living increase shall be an option for the LESSORS at the beginning of the second twelve-month option clause, which will be based on the national cost of living index, and shall not exceed 10%.

In consideration of this lease, the LESSEES will pay the LESSORS $ __150__ per month per stall leased, with an initial lease of___fifteen___ (_15_) stalls, and an option to lease the remaining ___fifteen___ (_15_) stalls at any time during the term of the lease. (Any outside paddock will be $_____ per month.) If a mare and a foal are both on board in a paddock or stall, there will be an additional $ __50__ per month charge for the foal after the weanling has reached the age of three months.

Until such time as the LESSEES exercise the option on the unused stalls, the LESSORS may use the stalls for their own personal use.

(Optional.) The LESSEES also agree to contract under a separate contract with the LESSORS to have the following services provided: 1) alfalfa hay and sweet grain supplied to the LESSEES' horses on a daily basis, and 2) the stalls cleaned and the necessary bedding provided on a daily basis. The LESSEES agree to pay the LESSORS the amount of $ __50__ per month per stall or paddock leased for the above described services.

4. Insurance.
The LESSEES agree to carry personal and property liability insurance in the amount of one million dollars ($ _1,000,000_) with the LESSORS named as additional insured.

In addition, the parties agree to negotiate as to whether the necessity exists for the LESSEES also to carry workman's compensation insurance covering all persons employed in connection with the work and with respect to whom death or bodily injury claims could be asserted against LESSORS or the premises.

The LESSEES do / do not agree to carry workman's compensation insurance. (Circle, initial, and date the applicable choice.)

5. Utilities.

The LESSORS / LESSEES (circle appropriate one) agree to pay cost of utilities, including water, electricity, and waste disposal. (However, should utility use exceed the average monthly bill of $_____ , the LESSEES agree to pay the overcharge.)

6. Hold Harmless.

LESSEES hereby agree to hold LESSORS harmless from and against any and all claims, actions, damages, liability, and expense in connection with loss of life, personal injury, and/or damage to property arising out of the use of the property.

7. Default.

Upon material breach of this Agreement by one party, the other party may terminate same.

Upon any breach, the other party shall have the right to recover from said breaching party all reasonable attorney's fees and court costs.

8. (a) Governing Law.

This Agreement shall be governed by and in accordance with the laws of the State of_____ .
Any legal action must be brought in _____(county/municipality).

OR

(b) Arbitration.

The parties to this Agreement mutually agree that any and all disputes arising in connection with this Agreement shall be settled and determined by binding arbitration conducted in accordance with the then existing rules of the American Arbitration Association by one or more arbitrators appointed in accordance with said rules. Said arbitration shall take place in _____(municipality), _____ (state).

9. Entire Agreement.

This constitutes the entire Agreement between the parties. Any modifications or additions MUST be in writing and signed by all parties to this Agreement. No oral modifications or additions will be considered to be part of this Agreement unless reduced to writing and signed by all parties.

EXECUTED this <u>1st</u> day of <u>August, (year)</u> , at <u>Lexington, Connecticut.</u>

LESSORS	LESSEES
_____	_____
(Name)	(Name)
_____	_____
(Name)	(Name)
_____	_____
(address)	(address)
_____	_____
_____	_____
(phone)	(phone)

SAMPLE

FEED AND STALL CLEANING CONTRACT

(Optional)

THIS CONTRACT is entered into between ___John and Jane Horseman,dba Hilltop Stables_____, and _____Robert and Susan Rider_____ in regard to the graining and haying of horses which are either owned by or under the control of ___Robert and Susan Rider_____and which horses are stabled on the property leased by ___Robert and Susan Rider_____ from ___John and Jane Horseman, dba Hilltop Stables_____ as well as the cleaning of the stalls and/or paddock and the provision of necessary bedding for such stalls.

___John and Jane Horseman, dba Hilltop Stables_____agree to provide the following services:
  1) alfalfa hay and sweet grain is to be supplied to the horses on a daily basis, and
  2) the stalls and/or paddock leased by___Robert and Susan Rider_____ are to be cleaned as well as the necessary bedding provided on a daily basis.

___Robert and Susan Rider___ agree to pay ___John and Jane Horseman, dba Hilltop Stables_____the amount of $___50___ per month per stall leased for the above described services.

It is the understanding of the parties that___John and Jane Horseman, dba Hilltop Stables_____will provide their own employees to perform the above described services, and that these employees are not to be under the supervision or control of _____ ___Robert and Susan Rider_____.

THIS CONTRACT is subject to the Laws of the State of _____. Any legal action must be brought in _____(county/municipality).

EXECUTED this__1st__ day of __August, (year)__ , at _Lexington, Connecticut._

Entire Agreement.
  This constitutes the entire Agreement between the parties. Any modifications or additions MUST be in writing and signed by all parties to this Agreement. No oral modifications or additions will be considered to be part of this Agreement unless reduced to writing and signed by all parties.

_____   _____
John and Jane Horseman,   Robert and Susan Rider
dba Hilltop Stables

_____   _____
(address)   (address)

_____   _____

_____   _____
(phone)   (phone)

Glossary

The following is a list of financial and legal terms used in this book with their definitions. Note that the definitions are limited to the specialized uses of these terms in the context of this volume.

Aggregate Dollar Amount: The total amount, including interest or additional related costs.

Amortization Schedule: A reduction in a debt by periodic payments covering interest and part of principal.

Appraisal: The valuation or an estimation of value of property by disinterested persons of suitable qualifications.

Arbitration: The hearing and determination of a dispute or the settling of differences between parties by a person or persons chosen or agreed to by them in advance. Intended to avoid the formalities, delay, and expense of ordinary litigation. May be binding or non-binding.

Assigns: Persons who are given an interest or full ownership in a property by the owner usually through a will, trust, or as a gift.

Capital: Investment money, the amount invested in a business.

Consideration: Any payment received in the form of money, property, or services.

Covenant: To promise or to agree to something as in a contract.

Encumbrance: Any interest in property that might interfere with the sale of the property, as in a claim, lien, charge, or liability attached to and binding real property.

Hypothecate: To offer something as security as in to mortgage property.

Indemnification: The act of indemnifying or the state of being indemnified.

Indemnify: To compensate for damage or loss sustained, expense incurred; to secure against anticipated loss.

Investment Security: Any corporate bonds or corporate obligation secured by property owned by the corporation; a written obligation giving the holder the right to receive property not in his possession.

Leasee: A person to whom a lease is granted.

Legatee: A person who receives property under a will.

Lessor: A person who grants someone a lease.

Lien: A charge against or interest in property to secure payment of a debt or performance of an obligation.

Mortality Insurance: The policyholder is paid the value of the policy upon the death of the insured (horse).

Net Cash: The amount of money left over after all the bills have been paid.

Notice: The letter informing a person of a change in a contract or a problem concerning a contract or the date of a meeting.

Par Value: A dollar amount assigned to a share by the company.

Partnership Information Form (Form 1065): An annual information return stating all items of income and deductions. Also included are the names and addresses of all partners and the amount of each partner's distributive share that year.

Passive Activity: Businesses in which a person does not materially participate based on tests of hours spent. The IRS has devised seven tests to determine material participation. Some tests require only a minimum amount of work, in some cases just more than 100 hours annually.

Passive Activity Loss Limitations: Rules that limit the deduction of losses from a passive activity to offset income from other passive activities. The following are not considered passive income: salary, self-employment earnings from a regular job, interest, dividends, royalties, retirement income, or gains from the sale of stock or similar investment property.

Passive Activities: Include rental operations, income as a limited partner, and all businesses in which the person does not materially participate.

Profit/Loss: The difference between the cost of the horse and the amount you receive for the horse.

Pursuant: In agreement with or in accordance with.

Release and Hold Harmless: The giving up of a right, claim, or privilege by the person in whom it exists or to whom it accrues, to the person against whom it might have been demanded or enforced.

Syndication: A group of individuals or organizations combined or cooperating to undertake some specific duty, transactions, or negotiations.

Testamentary Disposition: Something received through a will or a trust at someone's death.

Title: The right to ownership, also the evidence of ownership.

Waiver (n.): A voluntary, intentional relinquishment of a known right.

Appendix:

Blank Forms

PARTNERSHIP AGREEMENT

THE PARTNERSHIP AGREEMENT is made this _____ day of _____ (month), _____ (year), by and between _____ and _____ .

EXPLANATORY STATEMENT

The parties hereto desire to enter into the business of _____
_____
_____
_____ .

In order to accomplish their aforesaid desires, the parties hereto desire to join together in a general partnership under and pursuant to any applicable state code.

NOW, THEREFORE, in consideration of their mutual promises, covenants, and agreements, and the Explanatory Statement, which is incorporated by reference herein and made a substantive part of this Partnership Agreement, the parties hereto do hereby promise, covenant, and agree as follows:

Section 1. Name.
The name of the partnership shall be _____ _____

Section 2. Principal Place of Business.
The principal place of business of the Partnership (the "Office") shall be located at
_____
_____
_____

Section 3. Business and Purpose.
3.1 The business and purposes of the Partnership are to _____
_____
_____
_____
_____
_____ .

3.2 The Partnership may also do and engage in any and all other things and activities and have all powers incident to the said acquisition, holding, management, sale, and leasing of the Property, or any part or parts thereof.

Section 4. Term.
The Partnership shall commence upon the date of the Agreement, as set forth above, and shall terminate pursuant to the further provisions of this Agreement.

Section 5. Capital Contributions.
5.1 The original capital contributions to the Partnership of each of the Partners shall be made concurrently with their respective execution of this Agreement in the following dollar amounts set forth after their respective names:
_____ $ _____
_____ $ _____

5.2 An individual capital account shall be maintained for each Partner. The capital account of each Partner shall consist of his or her original capital contribution, increased by (a) additional capital contributions made by him or her, and (b) his or her share of Partnership profits, and decreased by (i) distributions of such profits and capital to him or her, and (ii) his or her share of Partnership losses.

5.3 Except as specifically provided in this Agreement, or as otherwise provided by and in accordance with law to the extent such law is not inconsistent with this Agreement, no Partner shall have the right to withdraw or reduce his or her contributions to the capital of the Partnership.

Section 6. Profit and Loss.
6.1 The percentages of Partnership Rights and Partnership Interest of each of the Partners in the Partnership shall be as follows:
_____ _____
_____ _____

6.2 For purposes of Sections 702 and 704 of the Internal Revenue Code of 1986, or the corresponding provisions of any future federal Internal Revenue law, or any similar tax law of any state or jurisdiction, the determination of each Partner's distributive share of all items of income, gain, loss, deduction, credit, or allowance of the Partnership for any period or year shall be made in accordance with, and in proportion to, such Partner's percentage of Partnership Interest as it may then exist.

Section 7. Distribution of Profits.

The net cash from operations of the Partnership shall be distributed at such times as may be determined by the Partners in accordance with Section 8 of this Agreement among the Partners in proportion to their respective percentage of Partnership Interest.

Section 8. Management of the Partnership Business.

8.1 All decisions respecting the management, operation, and control of the Partnership business and determinations made in accordance with the provisions of this Agreement shall be made only by the unanimous vote or consent of all of the Partners.

8.2 The Partners shall devote to the conduct of the Partnership business as much of their respective time as may be reasonably necessary for the efficient operation of the Partnership business.

Section 9. Salaries.

Unless otherwise agreed by the Partners in accordance with Section 8 of this Agreement, no partner shall receive any salary for services rendered to or for the Partnership.

Section 10. Legal Title to Partnership Property.

Legal title to the property of the Partnership shall be held in the name of _____
_____
or in such other name or manner as the Partners shall determine to be in the best interest of the Partnership.

Section 11. Banking.

All revenue of the Partnership shall be deposited regularly in the Partnership savings and checking accounts at such bank or banks as shall be selected by the Partners.

Section 12. Books; Fiscal Year.

Accurate and complete books of account shall be kept by the Partners and entries promptly made therein of all of the transactions of the Partnership, and such books of account shall be open at all times to the inspection and examination of the Partners.

Section 13. Transfer of Partnership Interest and Partnership Rights.

Except as otherwise provided in Sections 14, 15, and 16 hereof, no Partner (hereinafter referred to as the "Offering Partner") shall, during the term of the Partnership, sell, hypothecate, pledge, assign, or otherwise transfer with or without consideration (hereinafter collectively referred to as a "Transfer") any part or all of his Partnership Interest or Partnership Rights in the Partnership to any other person (a "Transferee"), without first offering (hereinafter referred to as the "Offer") that portion of his Partnership Interest and Partnership Rights in the Partnership subject to the contemplated transfer (hereinafter referred to as the "Offered Interest") first to the Partnership, and, secondly, to the other Partners, at a purchase price (hereinafter referred to as the "Transfer Purchase Price") and in a manner as agreed.

Section 14. Purchase upon Death.

14.1 Upon the death of any Partner (hereinafter referred to as the "Decedent") the Partnership shall neither be terminated nor wound up, but instead, the business of the Partnership shall be continued as if such death had not occurred. Each Partner shall have the right of testamentary disposition to bequeath all or any portion of his Partnership Interest and Partnership Rights in the Partnership to a member of his immediate family or to any trust in which any one or more members of the immediate family retain the full beneficial interests.

14.2 The aggregate dollar amount of the Decedent Purchase Price shall be payable in cash on the closing date, unless the Partnership shall elect prior to or on the closing date to purchase the Decedent Interest in installments as provided in Section 19 hereof.

Section 15. Purchase upon Bankruptcy or Retirement.

15.1 Upon the Bankruptcy or Retirement from the Partnership of any Partner (the "Withdrawing Partner"), the Partnership shall neither be terminated nor wound up, but, instead, the business of the Partnership shall be continued as if such Bankruptcy or Retirement, as the case may be, had not occurred, and the Partnership shall purchase and the Withdrawing Partner shall sell all of the Partnership Interest and Partnership Rights (the "Withdrawing Partner's Interest") owned by the Withdrawing Partner in the Partnership on the date of such Bankruptcy or Retirement (the "Withdrawal Date").

Section 16. The Appraised Value.

The term "Appraised Value," as used in this Agreement, shall be the dollar amount equal to the product obtained by multiplying (a) the percentage of Partnership Interest and Partnership Rights owned by a Partner by (b) the Fair Market Value of the Partnership's assets.

Section 17. Notices.

Any and all notices, offers, acceptances, requests, certifications, and consents provided for in this Agreement shall be in writing and shall be given and be deemed to have been given when personally delivered against a signed receipt or mailed by registered or certified mail, return receipt requested, to the last address which the addressee has given to the Partnership.

Section 18. (a) Governing Law.

It is the intent of the parties hereto that all questions with respect to the construction of this Agreement and rights, duties, obligations, and liabilities of the parties shall be determined in accordance with the applicable provisions of the laws of the State of _____ .
Any legal action must be brought in _____ _____(county/municipality).
   OR
(b) Arbitration.
The parties to this Agreement mutually agree that any and all disputes arising in connection with this Agreement shall be settled and determined by binding arbitration conducted in accordance with the then existing rules of the Americn Arbitration Association by one or more arbitrators appointed in accordance with said rules. Said arbitration shall take place in _____(municipality) _____ (state).

Section 19. Miscellaneous Provisions.

19.1 This Agreement shall be binding upon, and inure to the benefit of, all parties hereto, their personal and legal representatives, guardians, successors, and their assigns to the extent, but only to the extent, that assignment is provided for in accordance with, and permitted by, the provisions of this Agreement.

19.2 Nothing herein contained shall be construed to limit in any manner the parties, or their respective agents, servants, and employees, in carrying on their own respective business or activities.

19.3 The Partners agree that they and each of them will take whatever actions as are deemed by counsel to the Partnership to be reasonably necessary or desirable from time to time to effectuate the provisions or intent of this Agreement.

19.4 This Agreement and exhibits attached hereto set forth all (and are intended by all parties hereto to be an integration of all) of the promises, agreements, conditions, understandings, warranties, and representations among the parties hereto with respect to the Partnership, the business of the Partnership, and the property of the Partnership, and there are no promises, agreements, conditions, understandings, warranties or representations, oral or written, express or implied, among them other than as set forth herein.

Section 20. Entire Agreement.

This constitutes the entire Agreement between the parties. Any modifications or additions MUST be in writing and signed by all parties to this Agreement. No oral modifications or additions will be considered to be part of this Agreement unless reduced to writing and signed by all parties.

IN WITNESS WHEREOF, the parties have hereunto set their hands and seals and acknowledged this Agreement as of the date first above written.

WITNESS: Percentage of
                            Partnership
_____   Interest and
                            Partnership
                            Rights

_____ (SEAL) _____%

Residence Address: _____

_____

_____

_____

_____

_____ (SEAL) _____%

Residence Address: _____

_____

_____

_____

IN WITNESS WHEREOF, I have hereunto set my hand and seal as of the date first above written.

WITNESS: _____

_____ (SEAL)

SYNDICATE AGREEMENT

AGREEMENT, made _____ (date), between the persons whose names and addresses are set out in the Schedule attached and who have subscribed for the number of units set forth opposite their names ("Owners").

RECITALS

The Owners desire to form a Syndicate to purchase the _____ _____ herein referred to as the "horse."

The Owners will pay the sum of $ _____ per unit. There shall be _____ units in this Syndicate. _____ , acting for this Syndicate, shall purchase the horse for the sum of $ _____ and will accept delivery of the horse.

Upon said purchase of the horse, the Syndicate shall be in existence for the ownership and management of the horse upon the following terms and conditions:

1. Ownership.

The ownership of the horse shall be _____ units, to be insured at a price of $ _____ per unit; each of the _____units shall be on an equal basis with the others, and only a full unit shall have any rights.

2. Location.

The horse shall be stabled at _____ _____ _____ subject to change by consensus, and shall be under the personal supervision of _____ _____ , as Syndicate Manager.

3. Manager's Duties.

Subject to the approval of the Partner(s), the Syndicate Manager shall have full charge of and control over the management of the horse and of all training matters arising out of this enterprise, subject to the approval of the Owners. She shall keep accurate account of all expenses. She shall exercise her best judgment in all training decisions.

4. Transferability.

Units may be transferred subject to the terms of this Agreement, provided, however, that each Owner shall have the first refusal to purchase any unit or units that an Owner may desire to sell.

5. Expenses.

Each Owner shall pay his proper share of the expenses of the Syndicate, including organizational, legal, accounting, board, advertising, veterinary, etc., proportionate to the number of units which he holds. Bills will be sent out monthly and are payable within ten days.

6. Liability of Manager.

The Syndicate Manager shall not be personally liable for any act or omission committed by her except for willful misconduct or gross negligence.

7. Insurance.

The Syndicate Manager shall be responsible for insuring the horse. The expense of the insurance shall be shared by the Partners in accordance with this Agreement.

8. Accounting.

The Syndicate Manager shall furnish each Partner periodically with a statement showing the receipts and expenditures and such other information as she may deem pertinent.

9. Special Meetings.

A special meeting of the Partner(s) may be called by either Partner at any time of mutual convenience with reasonable notice.

10. Active Participation.

Notwithstanding Manager's duties, each Partner shall materially and substantially participate in the day-to-day decisions affecting and relating to this joint venture and all management decisions relating to said horse.

11. Notices.

All required notices shall be effective and binding if sent by prepaid registered mail, telegram, cable, or delivered in person to the address of the respective Owners set out in the Schedule attached. Such address changes shall hereafter be designated in writing to the Syndicate Manager, addressed to: _____

_____

_____

12. Miscellaneous.

This Agreement, when executed by the Owners, shall constitute the Agreement between the parties, and shall be binding upon the Owners, their heirs, and assigns.

13. Liability.

This Agreement shall not be deemed to create any relationship by reason of which any party might be held liable for the omission or commission of any other party, unless otherwise provided.

14. Termination.

This Syndicate terminates on the sale of the horse at which time the Syndicate Manager shall furnish each Partner with an accounting. All income and expenses shall be shared in accordance with the proportionate ownership of units.

15. (a) Governing Law.

This Agreement shall be construed in accordance with and shall be governed by the laws of the State of _____ .
Any legal action must be brought in the county/ municipality of_____ .
   OR
(b) Arbitration.

The parties to this Agreement mutually agree that any and all disputes arising in connection with this Agreement shall be settled and determined by binding arbitration conducted in accordance with the then existing rules of the American Arbitration Association by one or more arbitrators appointed in accordance with said rules. Said arbitration shall take place in _____ (municipality), _____ (state).

16. Entire Agreement.

This constitutes the entire Agreement between the parties. Any modifications or additions MUST be in writing and signed by all parties to this Agreement. No oral modifications or additions will be considered to be part of this Agreement unless reduced to writing and signed by all parties.

IN WITNESS WHEREOF, we have executed this Agreement the day and date first above written.

_____
Signature

_____
Address

_____
Units Purchased

_____
Signature

_____
Address

_____
Units Purchased

THE ARTICLES OF INCORPORATION

FIRST: I,_____ , whose post office address is _____ _____, being at least eighteen (18) years of age, hereby forms a corporation under and by virtue of the General Laws of the State of_____ .

SECOND: The name of the corporation (hereinafter referred to as the "Corporation") is _____ _____ .

THIRD: The purposes for which the Corporation is formed are:
   (1) To conduct a riding stable including a lesson program, to maintain a sales barn, and to maintain a string of show horses for outside owners.
   (2) To do anything permitted by the appropriate laws of the state.

FOURTH: The post office address of the principal office of the Corporation in this state is_____ _____ . The name and post office address of the Resident Agent of the Corporation are_____ _____ . Said Resident Agent resides in this state.

FIFTH: The total number of shares of capital stock that the Corporation has authority to issue is_____ shares of common stock, without par value.

SIXTH: The number of Directors of the Corporation shall be increased or decreased pursuant to the By-Laws of the Corporation, but shall not be fewer than three unless:
   (1) there is no stock held but then no fewer than one; or
   (2) if no fewer than the number of stockholders.

SEVENTH: The names of the directors who shall act until the first meeting are _____ _____ .

EIGHTH: The following provisions define, limit, and regulate the powers of the Corporation, the directors, and stockholders:
   (1) The Board of Directors of the Corporation may issue stock.
   (2) The Board of Directors may classify or reclassify unissued stock.
   (3) The Corporation may amend its Charter to alter contract rights of any outstanding stock.
   (4) [Any other specific right can be enumerated here.]
   Any enumeration of rights is not meant to limit any powers conferred upon the Board of Directors under state statute now in force or in force in the future.

NINTH: Unless the Board of Directors states otherwise, no shareholder has special rights to buy, convert, or in any other way to acquire stocks.

   I sign these Articles of Incorporation this _____ day of _____(month), _____(year).

_____
Signature

APPRAISAL OF A YOUNG HORSE NEVER SHOWN

I am qualified to appraise the value of a horse in today's market. I have been buying and selling show hunters for the last twenty-five years and am considered an expert in the field.

    I have personally evaluated the horse described as follows within the last _____ (_____) days:

Name: _____

Age: _____

Breed: _____

Sex: _____

Size: _____

    This horse is owned by _____residing at _____
_____and said horse is being donated to_____
_____. Based on the soundness, size, disposition, and athletic ability of this horse, I would set the fair market value at_____
_____ (\$_____). This price is fair and reasonable given the market and demand for horses of this type.

    This appraisal price is an objective estimate to the best of my ability and knowledge on this
_____day of _____ (month),_____(year).

_____
Signature of Appraiser

BILL OF SALE

I, _____ , residing at _____

_____ , in consideration of _____

_____ ($_____) , hereby paid to me by_____ ,

residing at _____ , sell to

_____the following described horse:

Name: _____

Age: _____

Color: _____

Breed: _____

Sex: _____

Size: _____

I hereby covenant that I am the lawful owner of the horse; that I have the right to sell the horse; and that I will warrant and defend said horse against lawful claims and demands of all persons.

Executed this _____ day of_____ ,_____ (date), under the laws of the

State of _____ .

_____

Signature of Seller

CONSIGNMENT AGREEMENT

THIS AGREEMENT is made between _____, the "Consignor," residing at _____ , and _____, the "Consignee," residing at _____.

1. Description.
The Consignor owns a horse described in this section below:

    (a) Name: _____

    (b) Age: _____

    (c) Breed: _____

    (d) Sex: _____

    (e) Size: _____

    (f) Markings and color: _____

2. Purpose.
The Consignee is in the business of buying and selling horses as an agent. the Consignor desires to sell said horse. Consignee agrees to make his best effort to sell said horse on behalf of the Consignor.

3. Warranties.
The Consignee accepts said horse into his sales barn under the following terms:

    (a) _____

_____

_____

    (b) _____

_____

_____

    (c) _____

_____

_____

    (d) _____

_____

_____

4. Board.
In consideration of _____ per horse per month paid by Consignor in advance on the first day of each month, the Consignee agrees to board said horse until sold or this Agreement is terminated.

5. Commission.
At the sale of said horse, the Consignee shall receive a commission of _____% on all funds received. The Consignor shall receive the balance of all funds on the sale of said horse within 10 days. The Consignee shall charge _____ % late fee per month on any late payment.

6. Care of Horse.

(a) The Consignee agrees to provide normal and reasonable care to maintain the health and well-being of said horse. This care includes (i)_____ ,
(ii)_____ , and (iii) _____
_____ .

(b) Routine veterinary and farrier care are authorized with direct billing. Any extraordinary care requires the consent of the Consignor unless on an emergency basis.

(c) The following feed and supplements shall be fed daily:

Hay: _____   _____
Grain: _____   _____
Daily supplements:

            _____
            _____
            _____

(d) Exercise

Said horse shall be ridden or lunged by Consignee or a competent rider employed by Consignee at least _____ days a week.

The Consignee will show the horse to potential buyers under the following terms.

(1) _____
_____
(2) _____
_____
(3) _____
_____

7. Retention of Title and Assumption of Risk at Sale.

Consignor retains title to horse. The title passes from Consignor to Buyer, and Buyer may take possession only upon transfer of full consideration to Consignee. Consignor retains risk of loss until title and possession pass to Buyer on the above conditions. Buyer assumes all risk and costs at the point of said transfer and prior to the horse's release from Consignee's premises.

None of the above terms are subject to change without explicit written agreement by the Consignor.

8. Lien.

Consignee agrees to keep horse free and clear of all liens and encumbrances.

9. Attorney's Fees.

This Agreement is terminated upon a breach of any material term, and the wronged party has the right to collect all reasonable fees and costs from the breaching party.

10. Termination.

Either party may cancel this agreement prior to sale on _____ days written notice and final accounting thereto.

11. (a) Governing Law.

This Agreement shall be construed in accordance with and shall be governed by the laws of the State of _____ . Any legal action must be brought in the county/municipality of
_____ .

OR

(b) Arbitration.

The parties to this Agreement mutually agree that any and all disputes arising in connection with this Agreement shall be settled and determined by binding arbitration conducted in accordance with the then existing rules of the American Arbitration Association by one or more arbitrators appointed in accordance with said rules. Said arbitration shall take place in_____(municipality) _____ (state).

12. Entire Agreement.

This constitutes the entire Agreement between the parties. Any modifications or additions MUST be in writing and signed by all parties to this Agreement. No oral modifications or additions will be considered to be part of this Agreement unless reduced to writing and signed by all parties.

_____   _____
Date   Signature of Consignor

_____   _____
Date   Signature of Consignee

LIMITED POWER OF ATTORNEY

I, _____ , of _____ ,
do hereby execute this Limited Power of Attorney with the intention that the attorney-in-fact hereinafter named shall be able to act in my place for the purposes set forth herein.

Section 1. Designation of Attorney.

I constitute and appoint_____
_____to be my
attorney-in-fact to act for me, in my name, and
in my place.

Section 2. Effective Date of Power of Attorney.

2.01 This Limited Power of Attorney shall
be effective as of the date of its execution by
me, and shall remain effective unless same
revoked by me, until midnight on_____ .

2.02 This Limited Power of Attorney shall
not be affected by my disability, it being my
specific intention that my attorney-in-fact shall
continue to act as such even though I may not
be competent to ratify the actions of my attorney-in-fact.

Section 3. Powers.

3.01 My attorney-in-fact shall have all of
the powers, discretions, elections, and authorities granted by statute, common law, and under
any rule of court necessary to sell my _____
_____
_____
_____.
In addition thereto, and not in limitation thereof,
my attorney-in-fact shall also have the power set
forth below.

3.02 My attorney-in-fact may collect and
receive, with or without the institution of suit or
other legal process, all debts, monies, objects,

interest, and demands due to me pursuant to the
aforementioned sale.

3.03 My attorney-in-fact may endorse my
name for deposit into a savings, checking, or
money-market account of mine with respect to
sums payable to me pursuant to the aforementioned sale.

3.04 My attorney-in-fact may execute, seal,
acknowledge, and deliver any documents
necessary, advisable, or expedient with respect
to the aforementioned sale.

Section 4. Ratification.

4.01 I hereby ratify, allow, acknowledge,
and hold firm and valid all acts heretofore or
hereafter taken by my attorney-in-fact by virtue
of these presents in connection with the aforementioned contract.

AS WITNESS my hand and seal this _____
day of _____(month),
_____ (year).

WITNESS:

_____

_____
Signature   (SEAL)

AGREEMENT FOR SALE OF UNBORN FOAL

THIS IS AN AGREEMENT BETWEEN _____ , hereinafter referred to as "Buyer" and _____ , hereinafter referred to as "Seller," who is the sole owner of the mare, _____ , hereinafter referred to as "mare."

A foal is due to be born to said mare on or about the month of _____ by _____ [stallion's name and I.D.].

In consideration of the promises and of the recitals set forth herein by Buyer and Seller, Buyer hereby agrees to buy and Seller hereby agrees to sell the unborn foal upon the following terms and conditions:

1. Location, Cost of Care and Maintenance, Title.

(a) Seller will, according to the terms of this Agreement, board the mare and the foal at no cost to Buyer until such time as the foal is weaned (in no event earlier than five months after foal's birth) and possession of the foal is transferred to Buyer. The Buyer is responsible for all veterinary expenses for foal after _____ .

(b) Seller expressly promises and agrees that neither Seller nor anyone acting on Seller's behalf shall remove mare or her foal from _____ _____ unless and until both Buyer and Seller have given express written consent to the move.

(c) In which case, Seller shall give Buyer thirty (30) days written notice of any such proposed change of location during which time Buyer shall make all appropriate filings or recordings necessary to fully protect Buyer's interest in the foal; however, in no event shall the mare or foal be located outside of the United States of America or within any jurisdiction within the United States of America that has not adopted the Uniform Commercial Code.

(d) Seller does and shall retain full title to the mare; however, so long as the foal is in utero, Seller recognizes Buyer's interest in said foal and agrees not to transfer, lease, sell or in any way hypothecate Seller's interest in said mare. Seller further agrees that until the foal has been weaned, Seller shall not sell or in any way transfer or hypothecate Seller's interest in the mare to any other person.

(e) The term of this Sale Agreement as to the mare and foal shall begin on the date set forth herein and shall terminate when all conditions have been fulfilled and physical possession of the foal is given to Buyer.

(f) Seller agrees to provide and maintain a proper environment for the mare and foal with all stabling, turnout area, appropriate feed, constant supply of fresh water, veterinary care, and all other reasonable and necessary goods and services for the mare and foal until such time as the foal has been weaned and physical possession of the foal has been given to the Buyer.

2. Purchase Price.

Buyer agrees to pay to Seller _____ Dollars as follows:

(a) Upon the signing of this Agreement, Buyer tenders the amount of _____ _____ Dollars, the receipt and sufficiency whereof is hereby acknowledged by Seller.

(b) On or before _____(date), Buyer shall deposit in an escrow fund (such as an attorney's trust account) the amount which is the balance of the purchase price agreed upon.

(c) The above-referenced balance shall be paid out of the trust account to Seller upon the fulfillment of the following terms and conditions:

(i) Mare foals out.

(ii) The foal is pronounced live, healthy, and insurable by a doctor of veterinary medicine within _____ hours of foaling and a certificate of good health shall be signed and delivered to Buyer or Buyer's attorney by a doctor of veterinary medicine.

(iii) Buyer has received written confirmation of full all risk mortality and accident insurance on said foal in the full amount of the purchase price and the beneficiary of the insurance shall be Buyer herein and shall insure his interest in the foal for the full purchase amount; and the statement for the premium of said insurance policy shall be sent to Buyer for payment.

3. Conditions Precedent.

Buyer's obligations to deliver the balance of the purchase price shall be subject to the satisfaction of the following conditions precedent.

(a) Mare shall give birth to a live foal by_____ (Name of Stallion) on or about _____ (date), but in no event before_____ (date).

(b) Said foal shall remain alive and in good health for at least_____hours, be sound and be both insurable and, in fact, insured for the full purchase price against all risks, naming Buyer as beneficiary.

(c) Said foal shall have no_____ (state here any objectional markings peculiar to particular breed, but this condition precedent may be waived by Buyer at Buyer's sole discretion).

(d) The mare, _____ (Name of Mare), shall be taken to _____and shall remain at said location until the foal is weaned.

OR

Shall remain at_____ until the foal is weaned.

(f) All documents which are required by the _____ to effect transfer of the foal from Seller to Buyer have been executed by Seller and delivered to Buyer or Buyer's attorney. It is understood that should the _____ or any other entity or body require any other forms or certificates signed by Seller, Seller shall, within five (5) days of receipt, properly complete and execute and return all documents sent to Seller by Buyer.

(g) The unborn foal has not in any way been sold to or hypothecated to anyone other than Buyer herein.

(h) This Agreement and all other documents to be executed by Seller have been duly authorized, executed, and delivered by Seller and constitute valid, legal, and binding agreements enforceable in accordance with their terms.

(i) The entering into and performance of this Agreement and the documents to be executed by Seller will not violate any judgment, order, law, or regulation applicable to Seller or result in any breach or constitute a default under, or result in the creation of any lien, charge, security interest, or other encumbrance upon a foal pursuant to any indenture, mortgage, deed of trust, bank loan or credit arrangement, or other instrument to which Seller is a party or by which it or its assets may be bound.

(j) There are no suits or proceedings pending, or to the knowledge of Seller, threatened in any court or before any regulatory commission, board, or other governmental authority against or affecting Seller, which will have a materially adverse effect on the ability of Seller to fulfill his obligations under this Sale Agreement.

(k) There exists no defect or impediment on the registration of the mare with the _____ _____ , and the_____

will issue a certificate for the foal when born, showing that its sire is _____
and its dam is_____, and that foal is a duly qualified and registered
_____foal.

[Seller / Buyer] will pay registration fees.

4. Taxes.

Seller agrees to pay and to indemnify and hold Buyer harmless from all license and registration
fees and all taxes, including, without limitation, income, franchise, sales, use, personal property stamp,
or other taxes, levies and post duties, charges, or withholdings of any nature, together with any penalties, fines, or interest thereon, imposed against Seller by any federal, state, or local government or a
taxing authority with respect to the purchase, ownership, delivery, possession, use, or transfer with
respect to the foal. All amounts payable by Seller pursuant to this section shall be payable to the extent
not theretofore paid on written demand of Buyer.

5. Identification of Buyer.

Seller will, from the date of the signing of these documents to the date that physical possession of
the foal is delivered to the Buyer, clearly identify by appropriate markings and/or in any conversations
that the foal is owned by Buyer herein and Seller will expressly advise anyone who inquires or indicates any interest in either mare or the foal that Seller no longer has any interest in the foal and the fact
the foal is owned by Buyer.

6. Notice.

Any notice required or permitted to be given by either party hereto shall be deemed to have been
given when deposited in the United States certified mail, postage prepaid, and addressed to the other
party at the address where indicated on the last page of this Agreement, or addressed to either part at
such other address as such party shall hereafter furnish to the other party in writing.

7. Assignment.

Neither party shall assign this Agreement or their interest thereunder without the prior consent of
the other party.

8. Termination by Buyer.

In the event that any obligation of the Seller has not been met or if any condition precedent set
forth above has not been fulfilled, Buyer shall have the right to terminate this Agreement. Should Seller
fail to do so upon demand from Buyer, Seller agrees to pay all costs and reasonable attorney's fees that
Buyer may incur to collect said monies from Seller.

9. Default.

In case of default by the Seller, it is expressly agreed that Buyer may either revoke this Agreement
and demand an immediate refund of all monies paid plus interest at the rate of_____per annum,
or sue for specific performance and demand strict compliance by Seller with the terms of this Agreement, or any combination of the above and/or together with any and all remedies allowed by law. It is
specifically agreed by Seller that should Seller default, whatever remedy or combination of remedies
pursued by Buyer, Seller will pay as additional damages all costs, expenses, and reasonable attorney's
fees incurred by Buyer in enforcing his rights hereunder.

Should Buyer default, it is agreed by both parties that Seller may retain any deposit monies
tendered by the Buyer. The Seller must try to mitigate his or her damages by offering the unborn foal to
other sellers. However, in the event that Seller is unable to secure another buyer at the same or greater
price than the price originally agreed upon by the parties, the Buyer is responsible for the difference
between the contract price and the actual sales price plus any actual or consequential damages incurred
by the Seller.

10. (a) Governing Law.

This Agreement shall be construed in accordance with and shall be governed by the laws of the State of _____. Any legal action must be brought in the county/municipality of

_____ .

OR

(b) Arbitration.

The parties to this Agreement mutually agree that any and all disputes arising in connection with this Agreement shall be settled and determined by binding arbitration conducted in accordance with the then existing rules of the American Arbitration Association by one or more arbitrators appointed in accordance with said rules. Said arbitration shall take place in _____(municipality) _____ (state).

11. Liquidated Damages.

In the event of Seller's default in any of the provisions hereunder, it is agreed by the parties that Buyer's damages could vary widely and would be very difficult to ascertain. Therefore, the Buyer and Seller agree that should Seller default, Buyer has the option of demanding the sum of _____ _____ Dollars from Seller as liquidated damages for any of Buyer's claims hereunder. This option shall be of no force and effect unless and until Buyer specifically elects in writing to pursue this remedy. This provision is not provided as a penalty and it is specifically agreed that should this remedy be selected by Buyer and suit brought to enforce the terms contained herein, that Seller, in addition to_____Dollars of liquidated damages, will also pay all costs, expenses, and reasonable attorney's fees incurred by Buyer in enforcing this provision.

12. Entire Agreement.

This constitutes the entire Agreement between the parties. Any modifications or additions MUST be in writing and signed by all parties to this Agreement. No oral modifications or additions will be considered to be part of this Agreement unless reduced to writing and signed by all parties.

Dated: _____

Seller: _____

Buyer: _____

Buyer: _____

Address: _____

Address: _____

BILL OF SALE
WITH PROMISSORY NOTE

THIS BILL OF SALE, made this _____ , day of _____ , by and
between _____ , hereinafter called Seller, and _____
_____ hereinafter called Buyer.

    1. That in consideration of the payment of _____

_____

in cash and a _____ promissory note,
by the Buyer to the Seller, the receipt of which is hereby acknowledged, said Seller does hereby
bargain, sell, transfer, assign, and convey unto said Buyer, its successors and assigns, free and clear of
all debts, liens, and encumbrances, the horse as described below:

    A. Name: _____

    B. Age: _____

    C. Color: _____

    D. Breed: _____

    E. Sex: _____

    F. Size: _____

    2. The Seller hereby represents that said horse hereby sold is its horse and that title is vested and
that it has a good and perfect right to sell same, and that no debts, claims, obligations, or encumbrances exist on or against said horse.

    WITNESS, under the laws of the state of _____ , the hand of the Seller and Buyer.

WITNESS:

_____   _____

                                                                _____
                                                               Address

                                                               _____
                                                                Telephone

                                                                _____

                                                                Address

                                                                _____
                                                                Telephone

PROMISSORY NOTE

THIS AGREEMENT is made between _____ (the "Undersigned") and _____

1. Consideration

FOR VALUE RECEIVED, _____ _____ does hereby promise to pay to the order of _____ the sum of _____ _____($_____) Dollars, together with interest on the unpaid principal balance at the rate of _____ Percent (_____ %) per annum from the date hereof in installments beginning on _____ _____and on the first of each month thereafter in the amount of $ _____ until the entire principal balance is paid in full or until_____ thereafter, at which time the amount then owing shall be due.

2. Payment Terms

The monthly payments are calculated on an amortization schedule of _____ years and the full amount then owing shall be due_____ years from the date of the first payment, unless otherwise accelerated under the terms and conditions hereof. Both principal and interest shall be payable at the address of _____ at _____ _____ , or at such other address as may be designated from time to time by written notification to the Undersigned by the holder hereof.

3. Prepayment

The Undersigned shall have the right to prepay, at any time or times, without penalty, all or any part of the balance of the principal hereof. Any such prepayment shall be applied first to any unpaid interest accrued hereunder and then to the principal, in which case the amounts due with respect to succeeding interest payments hereunder shall be adjusted accordingly.

4. Default

In the event (any of which events shall be deemed an "event of default"): (a) the Undersigned shall fail to make any payment of principal or interest when due hereunder and such failure shall have continued for ten (10) days after written notice of such default by the holder hereof, or (b) any voluntary petition by, or involuntary petition against, the Undersigned shall be filed under any chapter of the Federal Bankruptcy Act, or any proceeding involving the Undersigned shall be instituted under any other law relating to the relief of debtors, and such petition or proceeding shall not be vacated within ten (10) days thereafter, or (c) the Undersigned shall make any assignment for the benefit of creditors, or (d) a judgment shall be entered against the Undersigned in any court of record and shall not be satisfied within five (5) days thereafter, then the holder hereof, in his, his/her, or their sole discretion may declare this Promissory Note to be due forthwith, and the same shall thereupon become immediately due and payable in full, all without any presentment, demand, or notice of any kind, which are hereby waived.

5. Rights of Holder

No delay or omission on the part of the holder hereof in the exercise of any right or remedy shall operate as a waiver thereof, and no single or partial exercise by the holder of any right or remedy shall preclude other or further exercise of any right or remedy.

6. Remedies

The Undersigned hereby authorizes any attorney of any court within the State of _____ or elsewhere to confess judgment against the Undersigned at any time after this Promissory Note is due (whether upon normal maturity or acceleration hereunder), hereby waiving all exemptions, for the principal amount of this Promissory Note and interest and attorney's fees and court costs. If this Promissory Note is referred to an attorney for collection, then there shall be added to the amount due and owing hereunder reasonable attorney's fees of not less than 15% or such amount as any Court in which an action is filed deems to be reasonable, plus costs of collection.

7. Waiving of Defenses

The Undersigned hereby waives presentment, demand, notice of dishonor, protest, and all other demands and notices whatsoever in connection with the delivery, acceptance, performance, and enforcement of this Note.

8. (a) Governing Law.

This Agreement shall be construed in accordance with and shall be governed by the laws of the State of _____ .
Any legal action must be brought in the county/ municipality of_____.

OR

(b) Arbitration.

The parties to this Agreement mutually agree that any and all disputes arising in connection with this Agreement shall be settled and determined by binding arbitration conducted in accordance with the then existing rules of the American Arbitration Association by one or more arbitrators appointed in accordance with said rules. Said arbitration shall take place in _____(municipality) _____ (state).

9. Entire Agreement.

This constitutes the entire Agreement between the parties. Any modifications or additions MUST be in writing and signed by all parties to this Agreement. No oral modifications or additions will be considered to be part of this Agreement unless reduced to writing and signed by all parties.

Executed this_____ day of
_____(month),
_____(year).

_____

_____
Address

_____

_____
Telephone

PURCHASE AGREEMENT

THIS AGREEMENT is made between _____, residing at
_____ ("Buyer") and
_____, residing at _____
_____("Seller") for the purchase described below:

Name: _____

Age: _____

Color: _____

Breed: _____

Sex: _____

Size: _____

1. Purchase Price
For the total sum of $_____ , Seller agrees to sell and Buyer agrees to buy said horse based on the terms to follow.

2. Payment Terms
The Buyer agrees to pay $ _____ , as a deposit on _____
_____ and the balance due of $ _____ on
_____
_____

3. Warranties
   (a) Seller covenants that he/she is the lawful owner of said horse; that he/she has the right to sell said horse; and that he/she will warrant and defend the horse against lawful claims and demands of all persons.
   (b) Seller makes no other promises, express or implied, including the warranties of fitness for a particular purpose unless further provided in this Agreement.
   (c) Seller warrants the following: _____
_____
   (d) Buyer waives any claim for damage should said horse fail to meet the above warranties at the time of delivery, unless such defect is discovered within _____ days from delivery to Buyer.

4. Transfer of Ownership
Once Seller has received payment in full, Seller shall transfer all owner and registration papers of the horse at his own expense to the Buyer.

5. Risk of Loss
Seller assumes all risk of loss until the Buyer takes delivery or until the Buyer begins transfer of the horse, whichever comes first.

6. (a) Governing Law.

The terms of this Agreement shall be governed by the laws of the State of _____ .
Any legal action must be brought in _____ county/municipality.

OR

(b) Arbitration.

The parties to this Agreement mutually agree that any and all disputes arising in connection with this Agreement shall be settled and determined by binding arbitration conducted in accordance with the then existing rules of the American Arbitration Association by one or more arbitrators appointed in accordance with said rules. Said arbitration shall take place in_____(municipality), _____(state).

7. Breach

Either party may nullify this Agreement if the other party breaches a material term of this Agreement.
The wronged party may recover reasonable attorney's fees and court costs.

8. Entire Agreement.

This constitutes the entire Agreement between the parties. Any modifications or additions MUST be in writing and signed by all parties to this Agreement. No oral modifications or additions will be considered to be part of this Agreement unless reduced to writing and signed by all parties.

Executed this _____ day of _____ (month), _____ (year).

SELLER: BUYER:

_____   _____
Signature   Signature

_____   _____
Address   Address

LEASE AGREEMENT

This Lease is made _____ (date) between _____
residing at _____ (hereinafter
referred to as "Lessor"), and _____, residing at _____
_____ (hereinafter referred to as "Lessee").

1. Term.

(a) The term of this Lease shall be for a period of one year, beginning_____ (date)
and ending no later than _____ (date), or as otherwise provided for herein.

(b) Lessee shall have the option to return the horse to Lessor prior to the end of the lease term,
should circumstances dictate and providing lease fees are fully paid up to the time the horse is returned.
In no case will any fees be refunded for unused lease time.

2. Description.

This Lease covers the horse(s) described in this section below.

A. Name: _____

B. Age: _____

C. Breed: _____

D. Sex: _____

E. Size: _____

3. Consideration/Payment.

Lessee shall pay a fee of _____ ,
payable as follows:

Payment	Date
$ _____	_____
$ _____	_____
$ _____	_____
$ _____	_____

4. Uses of Horse and Limitations.

Lessee covenants not to use the horse for any purpose other than set forth: _____
_____
_____

Lessor promises that said horse is capable and suited for said purpose. Lessor explicitly denies the
right to any other part for any sublease agreement, barring all other riders except the Lessee's instructor or chosen professional rider where appropriate.

Lessee shall not have the right to relocate the horse, except as is usual for competition purposes,
without the written consent of the Lessor.

5. Instructions for Care.

Lessee will follow all practices consistent with quality care _____
_____ at Lessee's own expense. Lessee shall provide all necessary
veterinarian and blacksmith needs at Lessee's own expense. In addition said horse requires:

(a) _____
(b) _____
(c) _____
(d) _____

[Grain rations and hay plus stall size can be stated here.]

6. Risk of Loss and Insurance.

(a) Lessee assumes risk of loss or injury to said horse(s), barring an act of the Lessor or Lessor's agent.

(b) Lessee shall at his/her own expense at all times during the term of this lease maintain in force a policy or policies of mortality and loss of use insurance written by one or more responsible insurance carriers acceptable to Lessor. A copy of said policy must be mailed to Lessor within a month of taking delivery of the horse.

The liability under such policy shall be not less than_____
_____ payable to the Lessor as sole beneficiary.

7. Ownership.

Lessor warrants that he/she owns said horse free and clear and has the right to execute this Lease.

8. Options.

(a) Lessee has the option to renew this Lease for an additional_____ (_____) months
if a request is made in writing _____days prior to the expiration of this Lease,
provided the horse is available for a lease.

(b) If horse is placed up for sale, the Lessee has the right of first refusal to purchase said horse
within_____(_____) months of the expiration of said lease for a price not to exceed

_____ .

9. Covenant Not to Encumber.

Lessee agrees not to encumber said horse(s) with any lien, charge, or related claim and to hold Lessor harmless therefrom.

10. Default.

Upon material breach of this Agreement, Lessor reserves the right to remove such horse without incurring any responsibility to Lessee.

This Agreement is terminated upon a breach of any material term and the other party has the right to collect all reasonable fees and costs from the breaching party.

11. (a) Governing Law.

This Agreement shall be construed in accordance with and shall be governed by the laws of the
State of _____ . Any legal action must be brought in the county/municipality
of _____ .

OR

(b) Arbitration.

    The parties to this Agreement mutually agree that any and all disputes arising in connection with this Agreement shall be settled and determined by binding arbitration conducted in accordance with the then existing rules of the American Arbitration Association by one or more arbitrators appointed in accordance with said rules. Said arbitration shall take place in _____ (municipality),_____ (state).

12. Entire Agreement.

    This constitutes the entire Agreement between the parties. Any modifications or additions MUST be in writing and signed by all parties to this Agreement. No oral modifications or additions will be considered to be part of this Agreement unless reduced to writing and signed by all parties.

Signed this_____ day of _____(month),_____(year).

LESSOR: LESSEE:

_____   _____
Signature   Signature

_____   _____
Address   Address

_____   _____
Telephone   Telephone

LEASE — BREEDING SERVICES OF A STALLION

Lease made _____ between _____, a corporation organized and existing under the laws of the State of _____, with principal place of business at _____, City of _____, County of _____, State of _____, herein referred to as Lessor, and _____ of _____, City of _____, County of _____, State of _____, herein referred to as Lessee.

    Lessor hereby leases to Lessee, who is engaged in the business of breeding horses for the show ring and hunt field, the below described stallion. In consideration of the terms herein set forth, the parties agree as follows:

1. Description and Delivery of Stallion.
    _____ agrees to deliver Lessor's Thoroughbred stallion ("Stallion") herein described to stand for breeding services at _____ _____ at the above described location.

Name	Age	Color	Size	Jockey Club Reg. No.

2. Term.
    The Term of this lease shall be for a period beginning_____, and ending no later than _____, or as otherwise provided for herein.

3. Payment.
    Lessee shall pay a fee of _____dollars ($ _____) for the stud services of Stallion, payable in_____(_____) installments of _____ _____dollars ($ _____). The payment schedule is as follows:

Date	Amount
_____	_____
_____	_____
_____	_____
_____	_____

    Payments not made within ten (10) days of due date will accrue interest on the unpaid balance at 12% per annum.

4. Care and Service by Stallion.

(a) Lessee agrees to provide adequate feed, water, shelter, care, maintenance, and veterinary care as required in a manner consistent with good Thoroughbred practices in the County of_____ _____ , State of _____ at Lessee's expense. This care includes annual vaccinations and regular shoeing and worming. Any specific provisions as to feed, stall size, and turnout follow:

(1)

(2)

(b) Lessee covenants that Stallion shall not service in excess of _____ (_____) mares during the breeding season herein described. Lessee will provide a written report of all breedings every sixty (60) days.

(c) Lessor reserves _____ breeding rights with no fee charged, other than boarding charges on the mares.

5. Uses of Stallion.

Lessee covenants not to use the Stallion for any purpose other than breeding as herein provided.

6. Assignment.

Lessee shall not assign this lease, or any interest herein, nor sublet Stallion or in any manner permit the use of the Stallion for any purpose other than as herein set forth.

7. Insurance.

(a) Lessee shall at his own expense, at all times during term of this lease, maintain in force a policy, written by one or more insurance carriers acceptable to Lessor which shall insure Lessor against liability for injury to or death of persons or damage or loss of property occurring in or about the premises on which the Stallion is used for breeding. The amount of coverage per person, per accident, and for property damage must be approved by Lessor. In addition he must receive a copy of said policy within ten days of its effective date.

(b) Lessee agrees to insure Stallion for the lease period with mortality or loss of use insurance purchased from a company, approved by Lessor, for the sum of $_____ , said insurance payable to Lessor as beneficiary.

8. Miscellaneous Expenses.

Lessee will be responsible to pay all expenses incidental to or consequential of leasing Stallion as if he/she owned Stallion for said term.

9. Permission to Inspect.

Lessor may inspect Stallion at any and all times, and Lessee agrees to follow strictly all reasonable instructions, regarding feed, care, handling, and breeding of Stallion.

10. Termination of Agreement.

(a) At termination for whatever reason, Lessee shall redeliver Stallion to Lessor at above described address at Lessee's expense.

(b) Agreement is terminated on fifteen (15) days written notice if there is a material breach of terms set forth herein.

(c) Any reasonable attorney's fees or court costs incurred as a result of such breach shall be paid by breaching party.

(d) Agreement shall be terminated upon presentation of evidence by a veterinarian that Stallion is unable to successfully impregnate mares for whatever reason. Lessee shall have no right to refund and all payments are still due and payable in a timely fashion.

11. Lessor's Lien.

Lessee grants Lessor a first lien on any foals produced under the terms hereof, under
_____ law for all unpaid charges on account.

12. (a) Governing Law.

All terms and covenants of this Agreement shall be enforced and constructed in accordance with
the laws of the State of _____. Any legal action must be brought in
_____(county/municipality).

OR

(b) Arbitration.

The parties to this Agreement mutually agree that any and all disputes arising in connection with
this Agreement shall be settled and determined by binding arbitration conducted in accordance with the
then existing rules of the American Arbitration Association by one or more arbitrators appointed in
accordance with said rules. Said arbitration shall take place in _____
(municipality),_____ (state).

13. Entire Agreement.

This constitutes the entire Agreement between the parties. Any modifications or additions MUST
be in writing and signed by all parties to this Agreement. No oral modifications or additions will be
considered to be part of this Agreement unless reduced to writing and signed by all parties.

IN WITNESS WHEREOF, the parties hereto have executed this Lease Agreement as of the day
and year above written.

LESSOR: LESSEE:

_____   _____
Signature   Signature

_____
Name of Stallion

_____
Registration Number

BREEDING CONTRACT FOR STALLION

THIS AGREEMENT is made by and between _____
_____ , residing at _____ ,
hereinafter referred to as "Owner of Stallion," and_____ ,
located at _____ , hereinafter referred to as "Owner of Mare."

1. Fees.

a. In consideration of_____Dollars
(plus applicable sales tax), Owner of Stallion hereby agrees to breed his stallion _____
_____ to _____ , a mare owned by _____
_____ .

b. Owner of Mare agrees to pay said $ _____ on the dates indicated below:

Date   Amount

_____   _____

_____   _____

_____   _____

c. In the event that Owner of Mare's mare does not take and become in foal, Owner of Stallion agrees to breed said mare again for $ _____additional consideration at any time prior to
_____ .

d. In the event said mare does not deliver a live foal, Owner of Stallion agrees to give Owner of Mare the right to an additional service to said mare (at any time within_____ months) from the last date of breeding said mare under this contract.

Owner of Stallion shall have no further liability hereunder for servicing said mare. For the purposes of this Agreement, "Live Foal" means "standing and nursing" for a period of at least
_____ .

2. Health/Other Requirements.

Owner of Mare warrants that said mare is free from disease or infection that could be transmitted to said stallion, and agrees to provide and pay for a veterinarian certificate, showing such freedom of disease or infection.

3. Boarding/Veterinary Care.

In addition to the above charge for breeding, Owner of Mare agrees to pay the following:
a. $15 a day for feed and board;
b. $10 a day for exercise of said mare as described below:
c. Owner of Stallion agrees to provide the following for the fees indicated;
    i. Feed:

            _____ of hay per feeding;
            _____ of grain per feeding;
            _____ feedings per day.

d. Stall:
Box Stall with outside paddock.

e. Turn-out/Pasture:
Daily turnout in pasture during first and second trimesters of pregnancy.

f. Owner of Stallion agrees to use reasonable care and caution for said mare while in his possession or control, pursuant to this Agreement, and is authorized to obtain any necessary veterinarian or farrier care as required, but only after taking steps to contact Owner of Mare without success. Owner is to provide local veterinarian of her choice and nearest veterinary hospital of her prior authorization to admit and treat said mare and to provide veterinarian and hospital with assurance of full payment for any and all treatment so made.

4. Liability.

Owner of Mare agrees to assume the risk of injury, sickness, or death to said mare except where caused by negligence of Owner of Stallion, his agents, officers, constractors, or employees.

5. Indemnification.

Owner of Mare agrees to indemnify and hold Owner of Stallion harmless for any loss or injury due to acts of said mare while on premises or under control of Owner of Stallion except where caused by negligence of Owner of Stallion, his agents, officers, contractors or employees.

6. Insurance.

To protect against said loss or injury, Owner of Mare agrees to secure liability insurance in the amount of $1,000,000 for personal injury per accident, and $500,000 per injury, and $300,000 property damage and to provide a certificate of insurance having named Owner of Stallion additional insured.

7. Rebreeding.

If prior to the breeding of said mare or after the mare has been bred but not come in foal, said stallion or mare dies or becomes unfit for service as so declared by a licensed veterinarian, then this Agreement shall become null and void and all monies paid by Owner of Mare, not including expenses, shall be refunded.

Or, mare owner shall have no right to a refund hereunder, but shall have the option of using the following stallions of the owner at the charges indicated:

_____

_____

8. Breeding Certificate.

Owner of Stallion agrees to execute all necessary documents of the registration of the offspring of the breeding and should he fail or be unable to do so, [Name of Agent if Registry permits] is hereby authorized to so execute on behalf of Owner of Stallion as his agent, only if the involved Registry will accept this agency appointment.

9. Termination.

Either party may terminate this Agreement for failure of the other party to meet any material terms of this Agreement. In the case of any default or breach by one party, the other party shall have the right to recover attorney's fees and court costs incurred as a result of said default.

10. (a) Governing Law.

This Agreement is governed and shall be construed under the laws of the State of _____.
Any legal action must be brought in _____ (county/municipality).

OR

(b) Arbitration.

The parties to this Agreement mutually agree that any and all disputes arising in connection with
this Agreement will be settled and determined by binding arbitration conducted in accordance with the
then existing rules of the American Arbitration Association by one or more arbitrators appointed in
accordance with said rules. Said arbitration shall take place in _____
(municipality), _____ (state).

11. Entire Agreement.

This constitutes the entire Agreement between the parties. Any modifications or additions MUST
be in writing and signed by all parties to this Agreement. No oral modifications or additions will be
considered to be part of this Agreement unless reduced to writing and signed by all parties.

Dated: _____ , _____ (year).

_____

_____
(Address)

_____

_____
(Address)

BREEDING CERTIFICATE

I, _____ , owner of the stallion named _____ ,
and described as follows:

Breed: _____
Description: _____

hereby certify and warrant that said stallion bred the mare named _____ ,
Registration Number _____ and owned by _____
which is described as _____
_____ , on the following dates and times:

Date: _____   Time: _____

Date: _____   Time: _____

Date: _____   Time: _____

Date: _____   Time: _____

I hereby agree to execute all necessary registration papers for any foal(s) both of said described
breedings and should I fail to do so I appoint [name of agent if allowed by Registry]
_____ as my agent who is authorized
hereby to execute said necessary papers based on the information set forth herein.

Date: _____ , _____ at _____

_____
(Signature)
(Owner of Stallion)

_____
(Address)

MARE LEASE AGREEMENT

THIS AGREEMENT is by and between _____ hereinafter referred to as "Lessor" and _____ hereinafter referred to as "Lessee."
   Lessor hereby leases to Lessee, who is engaged in the business of breeding _____ horses, the following mare:_____ (Name of Mare), a _____ (Breed), for breeding purposes by Lessee.

1. Term of Lease.

   The term of this lease shall be for approximately _____ , beginning _____ and ending when the foal to be received by Lessee herein has been weaned. Should Lessor leave the mare with Lessee beyond the term of this lease, and/or after at least ten (10) days written notice from Lessee that the mare is ready to be returned to Lessor, then Lessor shall pay the sum of $ _____ per day for feed and board to Lessee, plus necessary veterinary and farrier costs.

2. Lease Payments.

   Lessee agrees to pay the Lessor the following sums: $ _____ to be paid when said mare is pronounced in foal; $ _____ on or before _____ . Provided, however, if mare does not come into foal by _____ , Lessee, at his/her/ their option, may continue the lease on the same basis in _____ with no additional lease payments over and above those noted above, or he/she/they may terminate this lease and return said mare to Lessor and Lessee shall assume the costs of maintenance to day of termination as agreed to in Paragraph 3.
   If the mare is pronounced in foal, but a live foal is not born to said mare for any reason whatso- ever, Lessee may, at his/her/their option, renew this lease on the same terms in _____ , without additional lease payments, or in the alternative, terminate the lease and all monies paid shall be re- funded to Lessee. However, in either case Lessee shall assume the cost of maintenance to date as provided in Paragraph 3. "Live Foal" as used herein shall mean _____ _____ _____

3. Care and Maintenance.

   As further consideration to Lessor, Lessee promises that he/she/they shall assume the full care and maintenance of Lessor's horse during the term of this lease and agrees to provide reasonable breeding conditions and facilities, furnish proper feed, sufficient water, farrier care, adequate shelter, exercise, medical and veterinary care as required, in a manner consistent with good horse breeding practices in the State of _____ at Lessee's own expense as determined by Lessee. However, should Lessor have received the ten (10) day notice described in paragraph 1, then Lessor shall assume all the costs related to such care.

4. Risk of Loss/Insurance on Mare.

   Lessor shall bear all risk of loss from the death or harm to any of its mares unless such loss is caused by the gross negligence of Lessee, its agents or employees, in which case Lessee shall bear such loss. Lessee shall have no responsibility to maintain insurance on the life of the horse during the term of this lease.

5. Liability Insurance.

Lessee shall, at his own expense, at all times during the term of this lease, maintain insurance for injury to or death of persons or loss or damages to their property occurring in or about the premises on which Lessor's horse shall be used for breeding. Such insurance shall provide for $ _____ per injury, $ _____ per accident, and $ _____ property damage.

6. Use.

Lessee is authorized to use such mare for breeding purposes only.

7. Sublease/Assignment.

Lessee shall not assign this lease, or any interest herein, nor sublet said mare or in any manner permit the use of Lessor's mare for any purpose other than that which is set forth herein.

8. Indemnity.

Lessee agrees that he will indemnify Lessor against, and hold Lessor and Lessor's horse free and harmless from all liens, encumbrances, charges, and claims whether contractual or imposed by operation of law.

9. Permission to Inspect.

Lessee shall permit the Lessor to inspect the mare at any and all reasonable times after reasonable notice of Lessor's intent to do so.

10. Default.

If either party shall default with respect to any material condition or covenant hereof, by him/her/them to be performed, the other party may, but need not, declare this Agreement to be terminated. The breaching party shall be responsible to the other for reasonable attorney's fees and court costs related to any breach.

11. Waiver.

No delay or omission to exercise any right, power, or remedy accruing to either party on any breach or default of Lessee under this lease shall impair any such right, power, or remedy of said party, nor shall it be construed to be a waiver of any such breach or default, or an acquiescence therein, or in any similar breach or default thereafter occurring; nor shall any waiver of any single breach or default be deemed a waiver of any other breach or default theretofore or thereafter occurring. Any waiver, permit, or approval of any kind or character on the part of either party of any breach or default under this lease, or any waiver on part of the other party of any provision or condition of this lease, must be in writing and should be effective only to extent in such writing specifically set forth. All remedies, either under this lease or by law, or otherwise afforded to Lessor, shall be cumulative and not alternative.

12. Effect of Lease.

The provisions of this lease shall be binding on the heirs, executors, administrators, and assigns of Lessor and Lessee in like manner as on the original parties, unless modified by mutual agreement.

13. (a) Governing Law.

The parties agree that the terms of this lease shall be construed in accordance with and governed by the laws of the State of _____. Any legal action must be brought in _____ (county/municipality).

OR

(b) Arbitration.

The parties to this Agreement mutually agree that any and all disputes arising in connection with this Agreement shall be settled and determined by binding arbitration conducted in accordance with the then existing rules of the American Arbitration Association by one or more arbitrators appointed in accordance with said rules. Said arbitration shall take place in _____ (municipality), _____ (state).

14. Entire Agreement.

This constitutes the entire Agreement between the parties. Any modifications or additions MUST be in writing and signed by all parties to this Agreement. No oral modifications or additions will be considered to be part of this Agreement unless reduced to writing and signed by all parties.

Dated: _____ , _____

LESSOR: _____   LESSEE: _____

_____   _____
(Name)   (Name)

_____   _____
(Address)   (Address)

BREEDING CONTRACT FOR MARE

THIS AGREEMENT is made by and between _____ , residing at
_____ , hereinafter referred to as "Owner of Mare"
and _____ , a Missouri corporation, located at _____
_____ , hereinafter referred to as "Stud Farm."

1. Stallion and Mare.

Stud Farm is the owner of stallion:_____ , a _____-year-old,
_____ , tattoo #_____ , and Owner is the owner of the
mare named _____ , tattoo # _____ , described as a _____
_____ , foaled in_____ , by_____ , Reg. No._____ and, out
of _____ , due to foal _____.

2. Booking.

_____ will stand at stud during the _____ season at Stud Farm,
and the parties hereto desire to contract with Owner of Mare for one season's booking from
_____ for the services of the mare.

3. Fees.

It is agreed as follows:

a. Upon payment of _____ dollars booking fee, which is not
refundable, Stud Farm does hereby reserve for the Owner of Mare one season's booking from
_____ , for the services of the mare.

b. (i) The mare shall remain at the Stud Farm for a sufficient time to be pregnancy-checked after
having been bred.

(ii) Board at the rate of $_____per day for the keeping and ordinary care of the mare and/or foal
will be paid by Owner of Mare.

(iii) The balance of the Breeding Fee, $_____plus all unpaid board and expenses, will be
paid when the mare is picked up.

4. Health/Other Requirements.

a. All mares must be accompanied by a health certificate indicating current vaccination for equine
influenza (strangles, tetanus, and sleeping sickness are also recommended upon arrival at the Stud
Farm). Mares not accompanied by such certificate will be vaccinated shortly after arrival at expense
of Owner.

b. Stud Farm requires a negative Coggins Test for Equine Infectious Anemia (Swamp Fever)
prior to mare's arrival at Stud Farm.

c. Owner agrees to allow Stud Farm to have a qualified veterinarian check the mare for normal
breeding conditions, and to perform such other veterinary services that Stud Farm may deem necessary
for the proper treatment and protection of the mare and/or foal at side. Owner is responsible for said
services and expense and will be billed and will pay for said services before mare is picked up from
Stud Farm.

d. Mares that are not halter broken or cannot be hobbled will not be accepted.

5. Liability.

Stud Farm shall not be liable for any sickness, disease, theft, death, or injury which may be suffered by the mare and/or foal at her side or any other cause of action whatsoever arising out of this breeding contract during the time that the mare is in the custody of Stud Farm, except for any acts by the Stud Farm, its officers, agents, contractors, or employees that amount to gross negligence. Owner fully understands that Stud Farm does not carry any outside insurance on horse(s) that are in their possession for breeding and boarding of the mare or mares.

6. Insurance.

Owner of Mare shall maintain at his own expense insurance for injury to or death of persons or loss or damage to their property occurring in or about the premises of the Stud Farm for the term of this Agreement. Such insurance shall provide $_____ per injury, $_____ per accident, and $_____ for property damage. Owner must provide proof of such insurance.

7. Return Breeding.

Stud Farm guarantees a return breeding the following season provided the stallion is able to service mares either for said mare or an approved substitute should a live foal not result from this mating. For the purposes of this Agreement, a live foal shall be one that stands and nurses without assistance. This is to be evidenced by a written statement from a qualified veterinarian. In the event the stallion is not able to re-service said mare, Stud Farm may substitute another stallion at Owner of Mare's option or all monies paid by Owner of Mare for the previous service, not including expenses, shall be refunded to Owner of Mare.

8. Assignment.

This contract shall not be assigned or transferred by either party hereto without the consent of the other. If the mare is to be rebred and Owner of Mare fails to deliver her for breeding the following year, then any and all fees paid shall not be refundable and this contract is thereby canceled.

9. (a) Governing Law.

This Agreement shall be governed by and in accordance with the laws of the State of _____ _____. Any legal action must be brought in _____ (county/municipality).
OR
(b) Arbitration.

The parties to this Agreement mutually agree that any and all disputes arising in connection with this Agreement shall be settled and determined by binding arbitration conducted in accordance with the then existing rules of the American Arbitration Association by one or more arbitrators appointed in accordance with said rules. Said arbitration shall take place in_____ (municipality),_____ (state).

10. Entire Agreement.

This constitutes the entire Agreement between the parties. Any modifications or additions MUST be in writing and signed by all parties to this Agreement. No oral modifications or additions will be considered to be part of this Agreement unless reduced to writing and signed by all parties.

Dated _____

Stud Farm Owner   Owner of Mare

_____   _____

MARE INFORMATION FORM

Booked to _____(Name of Stallion's Farm)

Owner's Name: _____

Phone No.: _____

Address: _____

_____

Mare's Name: _____

Tattoo No. _____

_____

(Sire's Sire)

_____

(Sire)

_____

(Sire's Dam)

_____

(Mare)

_____

(Dam's Sire)

_____

(Dam)

_____

(Dam's Dam)

Foaled:_____Color: _____

Markings: _____

Anticipated arrival date at stud farm: _____

Foal at side: _____ Sire of Foal: _____

Date of last foaling: _____

Mare to remain at breeding farm until pregnancy check? Yes ____ No ____

Does Mare have any dangerous propensities? If yes, describe below.

Reproductive History of Mare:

Breeding History:

Date of last breeding: _____ Problems, if any: _____

Medications: _____

Hormones (F.S.H., L.H., Progesterone), if used: _____

Other: _____

Vaccination History:

Tetanus Toxois: _____ Date: _____

VEE: _____

Encephalomyelitis (sleeping sickness),
Eastern & Western strains: _____

Coggins: _____

Date of last worming: _____

Colic: _____ Frequency: _____

Founder: _____ When: _____

Allergies, if known: _____

Other: _____

Feeding Program:

Hay type: _____ Amount: _____

Grain type/s: _____ Amount: _____

Pellets:_____   Amount:_____

Known Allergies to feeds: _____

Special Care Requirement: _____

_____

_____

_____

Habits: _____

_____

Whom to contact in case of emergency, if owner cannot be reached:

Is the mare insured?   Yes _____   No _____

_____
Name of Insurance Company   Telephone No.

_____
Address

_____
Amount of Insurance

_____
Insurance Agent

BOARDING AGREEMENT

This Agreement is made _____ , between _____
(referred to as "Stable") located at _____
and _____ (referred to as "Owner") residing at _____
_____ , owner of the horse described in Section 2.

1. Fees.

(a) In consideration of _____ ($_____) Dollars per horse per month paid by Owner in advance on the first day of each month, the stable agrees to board said horse beginning_____ .

(b) Options to the basic fee paid in the same timely fashion are available as listed below. Each additional requested service must be circled and initialed by the owner. These options can be changed at any time Stable receives written notice from Owner. The fees are subject to change given _____ days written notice by Stable.

(1) _____ - $ _____

(2) _____ - $ _____

(3) _____ - $ _____

(4) _____ - $ _____

(5) _____ - $ _____

(6) _____ - $ _____

2. Description of the Horse(s).

Name: _____
Age: _____
Color: _____
Sex: _____
Breed: _____
Height: _____
Registration/Tatoo No.: _____

3. Turn-Out.

If no options are chosen, the Owner will be expressly responsible for all exercise, and it is understood that the horse will (will not) be turned out.

4. Standard of Care.

All care is provided by Owner.

OR

Stable agrees to provide normal and reasonable care to maintain the health and well-being of said horse.

Optional Special Instructions:

(a) _____

(b) _____

(c) _____

(d) _____

5. Risk of Loss/Hold Harmless.

[Add here Release and Hold Harmless clause in accordance with and using the language of the state in which the Agreement is made, if that state has passed an Equine Activity Liability Law.]

[If your state has not passed such a law, use the following clause: "Lessee agrees to hold Lessor harmless from any act of ordinary negligence of Lessor or any of his agents, contractors, or employees arising from any accident, injury, or damage whatsoever, however caused, to any person or persons, or to the property of any person, persons, or corporations occurring during such term of this Lease and arising out of the use or care of said horse."]

6. Indemnity.

Owner agrees to hold Stable harmless from any claim caused by said horse(s) and agrees to pay legal fees incurred by Stable in defense of a claim resulting from damage by said horse(s).

7. Emergency Care.

If medical treatment is needed, Stable will call Owner. In the event Owner is not reached, Stable has the authority to secure emergency veterinary and/or blacksmith care. However, Stable has no responsibility to pay for such emergency care. Owner is responsible to pay all costs relating to this care. Stable is authorized to arrange billing to the Owner, but Owner must make such arrangements with veterinarian and clinic in advance.

8. Shoeing and Worming.

Stable agrees to implement a shoeing and worming program, consistent with recognized standards. Owner is obligated to pay the expenses of such services, including a reasonable stable charge. Such bill shall be paid within fifteen days from the date the bill is submitted to Owner.

9. Ownership - Coggins Test.

Owner warrants that he owns the horse and will provide, prior to the time of delivery, proof of a negative Coggins test.

10. Termination.

Either party may terminate this Agreement. In the event of a default, the wronged party has the right to recover attorneys' fees and court costs, resulting from this failure of either party to meet a material term of this Agreement.

11. Notice.

Owner agrees to give Stable thirty (30) days notice to terminate this Agreement. The Owner cannot assign this Agreement unless the Stable agrees in writing.

12. Right of Lien.

Stable has the right of lien as set forth in the law of the State of _____ for the amount due for board and additional agreed upon services and shall have the right, without process of law, to retain said horse(s) until the indebtedness is satisfactorily paid in full.

13. (a) Governing Law.

This Agreement is subject to the laws of the State of _____. Any legal action must be taken in _____ (county/municipality). The parties have executed this Agreement this _____ day of _____, (year).
OR
(b) Arbitration.

The parties to this Agreement mutually agree that any and all disputes arising in connection with this Agreement shall be settled and determined by binding arbitration conducted in accordance with the then existing rules of the American Arbitration Association by one or more arbitrators appointed in accordance with said rules. Said arbitration shall take place in _____ (municipality),_____ (state).

14. Entire Agreement.

This constitutes the entire Agreement between the parties. Any modifications or additions MUST be in writing and signed by all parties to this Agreement. No oral modifications or additions will be considered to be part of this Agreement unless reduced to writing and signed by all parties.

STABLE:

Signed by: _____

_____
Address

_____
Telephone

OWNER:

Signed by: _____

_____
Address

_____
Telephone

TRAINING AGREEMENT

THIS TRAINING AGREEMENT (the "Agreement") made this _____ day of _____ _____ (year) , by and between: _____ , hereinafter referred to as "Owner," and_____ and _____ , hereinafter referred to as "Trainer."

    WITNESSETH that Owner owns the below described horse(s) and covenants with Trainer to train said horse(s) for the purpose and under the terms hereto agreed as follows:

1. Description of Horse and Delivery.
    Trainer agrees to arrange transportation to _____ on or about _____at Owner's expense the following described horse(s):

Name of Horse	Age	Color	Sex	Breed
1.				
2.				
3.				
4.				

2. Training Fee and Terms of Payment.
    Owner shall pay a fee of _____ Dollars ($ _____) per day per horse, payable as follows:

    (a) Each payment to be due and payable by the first of each month.

    (b) Any payment not received by the seventh of each month shall incur interest at 12% per annum for the number of days past the first.

    (c) Payment not received by the fifteenth of each month is subject to a $15.00 penalty charge over and above the monthly bill.

3. Additional Expenses.
    Owner shall be responsible for all costs directly related to this Agreement, including but not limited to transportation, veterinary bills, entries, grooming fees, and necessary special equipment. Owner will not be responsible for additional expenses exceeding_____ Dollars ($_____) per month without prior written approval. All additional expenses are due and payable on the first of the month as provided by Section 2.

4. Trainer Responsibilities.
    (a) Trainer shall fulfill the duties in a manner consistent with good show training practices in this County of _____ in the State of _____:

    1.

    2.

(b) Trainer shall pay all expenses according to Section 2, sending Owner an accounting each month.

In the event Trainer is not reimbursed on time, Trainer is authorized to deduct said payments from any other source available to Trainer.

(c) Trainer shall obtain all necessary veterinary and farrier services and as agent may authorize direct billing to the Owner. Any extraordinary care over and beyond normal and regular maintenance requires prior written approval by Owner unless involving the most immediate emergency treatment.

5. Showing.

(a) Any prize money won by Owner's horse while under this Agreement shall be treated as follows:

   1.

   2.

(b) Owner's horse(s) shall be shown in name of _____ with _____ as Owner and _____as Trainer.

6. Lay-ups.

If said horse(s) is out of training for more than _____ days consecutively, Owner shall pay the cost of board at _____Dollars ($ _____) per day plus incidental expenses as required. Owner must be notified within_____ (_____) days if horse is taken out of training.

7. Term and Termination.

(a) The term of this Agreement shall be _____ basis. Either party may terminate Agreement given _____(_____) days written notice, provided a final accounting by the Trainer is presented and all payments have been made by Owner prior to taking possession of said horse(s).

(b) On termination, Trainer shall have a lien on said horse(s) under_____law for all unpaid charges on account. Payment must be made in full before said horse(s) is released unless Trainer consents in writing.

8. Insurance.

(a) Owner shall bear all risk of loss from the death of or any harm to said horse(s) unless such loss is caused by gross negligence of Trainer, his agents, contractors, or employees, in which case Trainer shall bear such loss.

(b) Trainer agrees/does not agree to carry insurance protecting Owner against any losses caused by negligence of Trainer, his agents and employees.

(c) Owner agrees to reimburse Trainer _____% of the premium for said insurance.

(d) Trainer agrees/does not agree to maintain liability insurance.

   1. $_____ per person
   2. $_____ per accident
   3. $_____ property damage

If insurance is so provided, Trainer will make a copy of the policy available to Owner.

9. Indemnification.

Owner agrees to indemnify Trainer unless otherwise provided by insurance against all liability or claims, demands, and costs for or arising out of this Agreement unless such are caused by the gross negligence of Trainer, his agents, contractors, or employees.

10. Binding Effect.

(a) The parties hereto agree that this Agreement shall be binding on their respective heirs, successors, and assigns.

(b) Failure of either party to abide by and perform any and all other terms, covenants, conditions, and obligations of this Agreement shall constitute a default and shall, in addition to any other remedies provided by law or in equity, entitle the wronged party to reasonable attorneys' fees and court costs related to such breach.

11. (a) Governing Law.

This Agreement shall be governed by and in accordance with the laws of the State of_____
_____ . Any legal action must be brought in _____
(county/municipality).

OR

(b) Arbitration.

The parties to this Agreement mutually agree that any and all disputes arising in connection with this Agreement will be settled and determined by binding arbitration conducted in accordance with the then existing rules of the American Arbitration Association by one or more arbitrators appointed in accordance with said rules. Said arbitration shall take place in _____
(municipality), _____ (state).

12. Entire Agreement.

This constitutes the entire Agreement between the parties. Any modifications or additions MUST be in writing and signed by all parties to this Agreement. No oral modifications or additions will be considered to be part of this Agreement unless reduced to writing and signed by all parties.

IN WITNESS WHEREOF, the parties have executed this Agreement on the day and year first above written.

OWNER: TRAINER:

_____   _____
Signature   Signature

_____   _____
Address   Address

_____   _____

_____   _____
Telephone   Telephone

TRAINING AGREEMENT FOR RACEHORSE

THIS AGREEMENT is made on _____ between
_____ , located at
_____ herein called "Owner,"
and _____ residing at _____
herein called "Trainer."

    Owner is the legal owner of certain thoroughbred horses described below bred for racing and is desirous of having these horses trained and raced. Trainer is a Thoroughbred racehorse trainer and desirous of training and racing these horses.

    In consideration of the promises and agreements herein set forth, the parties agree as follows:

1. Description/Delivery of Horses.

Owner agrees to deliver the following horses to trainer to be trained and raced at _____
_____ (or at racetracks throughout the State of
_____ as the case may be):

Name of Horse	Age	Color & Sex	Jockey Club Registration No.

2. Training Fees.

    a. Owner agrees to pay Trainer _____ Dollars per day per horses trained and /or raced, subject to the provisions of Section 6. This daily charge shall be payable on or before the _____ day of each month.

    b. In the event that any of Owner's horses win a race, Owner shall allocate ten (10) percent from Owner's share of the purse money and said ten percent shall be paid to Trainer over and above any compensation as set forth in **(a)** above.

    c. In addition, Owner shall deduct another ten (10) percent from such purse money to be paid to the jockey riding the Owner's horse in the winning race.

    d. No deductions shall be made nor any monies paid to Trainer or the jockey from purse money received by the Owner as compensation for Owner's horse finishing in any other position than the winning position.

3. Duties of Trainer.

    Trainer shall train and race the horses and feed and care for them, subject to Section 4 herein, in a manner consistent with accepted horse training practices in the State of_____.
Trainer, in his sole discretion, shall decide when any of Owner's horses are sufficiently trained to be

entered in a race, and Trainer has sole discretion to decide what type of race any horse may be entered in and how often each horse should be raced, except that Trainer shall not enter any of Owner's horses in any claiming race for the sum of $_____Dollars or less without prior consent of Owner.

4. Expenses.

Owner shall bear the cost of transporting the horses from one track to another or otherwise, veterinary and medical costs, costs of preparation of racing silks, jockey fees, pony leads, and/or any costs of equipment that Trainer may deem necessary to the proper training and racing of any of Owner's horses, in addition to insurance costs as set forth in Section 8 below.

5. Accounting and Billing by Trainer.

Trainer shall pay all expenses referred to in Section 4, keep an accurate account thereof, and bill Owner for the same at the end of each month. If Owner fails to reimburse Trainer for such expenses when payable, Trainer is authorized to deduct an amount equal to such expenses from Owner's account from the Horsemen's Bookkeeper at the race track where Owner's horses are being trained and raced, pursuant to the limited power of attorney set forth in connection with this Agreement and incorporated herein by reference.

6. Horses Out of Training.

If, during the term of this Agreement, any of Owner's horses are taken out of training after being put into training, Owner shall pay the costs of boarding, feeding, veterinarian services and medicine, and transportation in maintaining any such horse, but shall not pay Trainer compensation for training as hereinabove set forth. Trainer shall notify Owner as soon as it is known that horse is or has been removed from training, and Owner shall pay thereafter $_____Dollars per day until the horse can be returned to training or can no longer remain at the track.

7. Amendment/Additions.

This Agreement may be amended at any time by writing into the provisions herein set forth the description of any additional racing stock desired by both parties to be placed within the terms of this Agreement, and the amendment shall be initialed by both parties.

8. Insurance and Indemnification.

a) **Insurance**. Upon receipt of the horses herein described, Trainer shall procure Thoroughbred racehorse insurance protecting Owner against any losses due to fire, theft, death, or other disability arising from any injuries of accidents to said horses, such insurance to provide coverage in an amount not less than $_____Dollars. Owner agrees to reimburse Trainer for such insurance costs in the manner set forth in Section 5 above.

b) **Indemnification.** Trainer agrees to indemnify Owner from all liability or claims, demands, damages, and costs for or arising out of the training and racing of Owner's horses, whether it be caused by the negligence of Trainer, his agents, contractors, or employees, or otherwise.

9. Termination.

If this Agreement is terminated for any reason prior to the expiration thereof, Trainer shall immediately deliver any horses under this Agreement to Owner at Owner's/Trainer's expense.

10. (a) Governing Law.

This Agreement shall be governed by and in accordance with the laws of the State of _____ . Any legal action must be brought in _____ (county/municipality).

OR

(b) Arbitration.

The parties to this Agreement mutually agree that any and all disputes arising in connection with this Agreement shall be settled and determined by binding arbitration conducted in accordance with the then existing rules of the American Arbitration Association by one or more arbitrators appointed in accordance with said rules. Said arbitration shall take place in _____ (municipality), _____ (state).

11. Entire Agreement.

This constitutes the entire Agreement between the parties. Any modifications or additions MUST be in writing and signed by all parties to this Agreement. No oral modifications or additions will be considered to be part of this Agreement unless reduced to writing and signed by all parties.

DATED: _____

_____   _____
(Name - Owner)   (Name - Trainer)

_____   _____
(Address)   (Address)

_____   _____

LEASE OF BOARDING
AND TRAINING FACILITY

1. Parties.

THIS AGREEMENT is entered into between _____
_____ , hereinafter referred to as "LESSORS," and
_____ , hereinafter referred to as "LESSEES."

2. Subject of Lease.

The property to be leased consists of the _____(_____)-stall barn, acreage, and
facilities commonly known as_____ located at
_____ .

The property, as described above, also includes, but is not limited to _____
_____
_____

(include all fixtures, etc.,) all of which are to be contained within the terms of this lease Agreement.

3. Terms of Lease.

This lease shall commence on _____and terminate on
_____ , for a period of _____months. At the end of the first
term, the LESSEES have the option to renew the lease for the further period of twelve (12) months by
advising LESSORS in writing at any time prior to ninety (90) days prior to the expiration of this lease.
A yearly cost of living increase shall be an option for the LESSORS at the beginning of the second
twelve-month option clause, which will be based on the national cost of living index, and shall not
exceed 10%.

In consideration of this lease, the LESSEES will pay the LESSORS $_____ per month per
stall leased, with an initial lease of_____(_____) stalls, and an option to lease the
remaining _____(_____) stalls at any time during the term of the lease. (Any outside
paddock will be $ _____ per month.) If a mare and a foal are both on board in a paddock or
stall, there will be an additional $_____ per month charge for the foal after the weanling has
reached the age of three months.

Until such time as the LESSEES exercise the option on the unused stalls, the LESSORS may use
the stalls for their own personal use.

(Optional.) The LESSEES also agree to contract under a separate contract with the LESSORS to
have the following services provided: 1) alfalfa hay and sweet grain supplied to the LESSEES' horses
on a daily basis, and 2) the stalls cleaned and the necessary bedding provided on a daily basis. The
LESSEES agree to pay the LESSORS the amount of $ _____ per month per stall or paddock
leased for the above described services.

4. Insurance.

The LESSEES agree to carry personal and property liability insurance in the amount of
_____($ _____) with the LESSORS named as additional
insured.

In addition, the parties agree to negotiate as to whether the necessity exists for the LESSEES also to carry workman's compensation insurance covering all persons employed in connection with the work and with respect to whom death or bodily injury claims could be asserted against LESSORS or the premises.

The LESSEES do / do not agree to carry workman's compensation insurance. (Circle, initial, and date the applicable choice.)

5. Utilities.

The LESSORS / LESSEES (circle appropriate one) agree to pay cost of utilities, including water, electricity, and waste disposal. (However, should utility use exceed the average monthly bill of $_____ , the LESSEES agree to pay the overcharge.)

6. Hold Harmless.

LESSEES hereby agree to hold LESSORS harmless from and against any and all claims, actions, damages, liability, and expense in connection with loss of life, personal injury, and/or damage to property arising out of the use of the property.

7. Default.

Upon material breach of this Agreement by one party, the other party may terminate same.

Upon any breach, the other party shall have the right to recover from said breaching party all reasonable attorney's fees and court costs.

8. (a) Governing Law.

This Agreement shall be governed by and in accordance with the laws of the State of_____ .
Any legal action must be brought in _____(county/municipality).
OR
(b) Arbitration.

The parties to this Agreement mutually agree that any and all disputes arising in connection with this Agreement shall be settled and determined by binding arbitration conducted in accordance with the then existing rules of the American Arbitration Association by one or more arbitrators appointed in accordance with said rules. Said arbitration shall take place in _____(municipality), _____ (state).

9. Entire Agreement.

This constitutes the entire Agreement between the parties. Any modifications or additions MUST be in writing and signed by all parties to this Agreement. No oral modifications or additions will be considered to be part of this Agreement unless reduced to writing and signed by all parties.

EXECUTED this _____ day of _____ , at _____

LESSORS	LESSEES
_____	_____
(Name)	(Name)
_____	_____
(Name)	(Name)
_____	_____
(address)	(address)
_____	_____
(phone)	(phone)

FEED AND STALL CLEANING CONTRACT

(Optional)

THIS CONTRACT is entered into between _____
_____ , and _____
in regard to the graining and haying of horses which are either owned by or under the control of
_____ and which horses are stabled on the property leased by
_____ from _____
_____ as well as the cleaning of the stalls and/or paddock and the
provision of necessary bedding for such stalls.

_____ agree to provide the
following services:

    1) alfalfa hay and sweet grain is to be supplied to the horses on a daily basis, and

    2) the stalls and/or paddock leased by_____ are to be
cleaned as well as the necessary bedding provided on a daily basis.

_____ agree to pay _____
_____ the amount of $_____ per month per stall leased for
the above described services.

    It is the understanding of the parties that _____
_____will provide their own employees to perform the above described
services, and that these employees are not to be under the supervision or control of _____
_____ .

THIS CONTRACT is subject to the Laws of the State of _____. Any legal
action must be brought in_____(county/municipality).

EXECUTED this_____ day of_____ , at _____

Entire Agreement.
    This constitutes the entire Agreement between the parties. Any modifications or additions MUST
be in writing and signed by all parties to this Agreement. No oral modifications or additions will be
considered to be part of this Agreement unless reduced to writing and signed by all parties.

_____   _____

_____   _____
(address)   (address)

_____   _____

_____   _____
(phone)   (phone)